What I Saw in Kaffir-Land

What I Saw in Kaffir-Land

Experiences with 'The Waterkloof Rangers'
During the Xhosa Wars in Cape Colony

Sir Stephen Lakeman
Mazhar Pacha

LEONAUR

What I Saw in Kaffir-Land
Experiences with 'The Waterkloof Rangers'
During the Xhosa Wars in Cape Colony
by Sir Stephen Lakeman
Mazhar Pacha

First published under the title
What I Saw in Kaffir-Land

Leonaur is an imprint of Oakpast Ltd

Copyright in this form © 2011 Oakpast Ltd

ISBN: 978-0-85706-663-3 (hardcover)
ISBN: 978-0-85706-664-0 (softcover)

http://www.leonaur.com

Publisher's Notes

Contents

Preface

This book contains extracts from the daily record of impressions made on my mind, by men and events, as we performed together our allotted parts, in one short tragical episode at the Cape. Very little has been omitted; nothing has been added. It is a simple narrative, taken from the *Book of my Life*, of which, if it is not the opening chapter, it is at least one of the first.

If by my observations I have hurt anyone's feelings, this may have been caused by these persons having ruffled mine. If I have said but little good of anyone with whom I have been brought into contact, it is because I failed to perceive any more than I have mentioned. The reader will be able to some extent to judge whether or not this has arisen from my want of perspicacity, or from their incapacity.

I can only add, that this narrative is true. I have thought, in having it published, that it might interest those who seek by reading some information about the realities of life in this artificial world of ours, wherein time-serving hypocrites present themselves so often as shams when Heaven and country call for men.

Militia est potior. Quid enim?

CHAPTER 1

Start for the Cape

In the year 1847 I was attached to the French staff in Algeria, and during several expeditions, both against Arabs and Kabyles, I became deeply impressed with the great superiority of the Minie rifle over the old smooth-bore. On my return to England I did all I could to enforce on the military authorities the advantages of this new weapon.

The Duke of Wellington gave me to understand, in several interviews he honoured me with, that he was perfectly satisfied as to the principle on which the Minie was constructed, but hesitated in giving effect to this opinion, on the conviction that the rapid twist of the rifling would so increase the recoil as to render this new weapon useless to the British soldier.

His Grace frequently observed, "Englishmen take aim, Frenchmen fire anyhow;" and no man could stand fairly up to harder kicking than old Brown Bess already gave.

General Browne, to whom the Duke handed me over for any further information I might have to impart, thought, after lengthened investigation, that the weapon was a good one for taking long shots from ramparts, but scouted the idea that it would ever be useful for active service in the field.

Colonel Airey, to whom General Browne confided me, asked if the Duke had really examined the gun; and on my assuring him that he had done so on several occasions, expressed his surprise at his Grace's having had so much patience. This naturally brought my interviews to a close with the military authorities.

Shortly afterwards the war broke out at the Cape, and the British army was, as usual, being kneaded into shape. The process, however, was so disintegrating, that the authorities at home were anxiously looking out for fresh food for powder. I therefore volunteered my services, under the condition that the men that served under me should have the Minie rifle. After much consideration, I was kindly told that I might order two hundred rifles at my own expense; and the military authorities would allow me to enlist two hundred volunteers—also at my own expense—and afterwards give us a free passage to the Cape, to go and shoot, and be shot at by, the *Kafirs*.

I accepted the offer as to the rifles, but declined to enlist the men in England. I need not say, that having no staff to aid me in enlisting, and no barracks to put the men in, the task was impossible. It was finally agreed that I was to engage the men at the Cape, and clothe them, the Government giving rations and pay as in the army.

I at once ordered fifty double-barrelled rifles of Messrs Barnett & Sons, Tower Hill, London, and one hundred and fifty single barrels on the same principle, of Messrs Hall, Birmingham. The rifles were soon ready; but the military authorities insisted on lengthy trials to burst them—to prove, I suppose, that they would be more dangerous to those who used them than to those they were used against. The cartridges also underwent innumerable trials: it was supposed by long-headed gentlemen at Woolwich, that the iron caps in the base of the bullets might be so struck that a spark could be emitted, the cartridge explode, and the engineer be hoisted by his own petard.

Colonel P—— of the 12th gravely surmised the possibility of one man communicating the danger to another; upon which Mr Jeffrey, of marine-blue fame, laughingly remarked that the battalion in that case would begin file-firing by shooting themselves off instead of their firelocks. These, and other equally reasonable suppositions, kept me in England, until I began to fear, from the accounts of slaughter sent home, that there would not be a *Kaffir* left to try my guns upon. However, as I knew from experience that despatches intended for a public a long way off were apt to be put in a very trumpet-speaking style, and how that through a little bit of brass a little puff can make a big noise, I started for the Cape in the good ship *Harbinger*, still in the hopes of proving the usefulness of this new weapon.

Chapter 2

Arrive at Sierra Leone

In the same ship were the newly-appointed Governor of the Cape, Mr Darling, and a Mr Macdonald, also recently appointed to the Gambia. The voyage was pleasant on all sides—ship, sea, and passengers—until we put into the Isle of St Vincent for coal. Here an event occurred which I should not relate had I been merely recording the actions of those around me; but I write these pages that others may learn the impulses that guide fellow-beings, who, from one cause or another, have in turn influenced many. As the ship was being coaled I had landed alone, and wandered about, gun in hand, to shoot, if I could, some snipe that were supposed now and again to visit the island. I could see nothing remarkable in this elevated spot but its geographical situation in the volcanic chain that runs from New Granada to St Eustache.

As for the snipe, I had not the courage to fire at a poor solitary wanderer like myself that rose at my feet; so, towards evening, I returned to the ship, tired with my walk on this torrid, brick-kiln-looking island, that rose in layers to the clouds like an altar of earth's burnt-offering reeking to the skies.

I had lain down in my berth, and had dozed off into dreamland, and fancied I saw a woman standing, much as the Virgin in Raffaele's "Assumption" at Dresden, high up between the ship and the shore, motioning me not to be afraid. At this moment down rushed the governor of the Gambia, exclaiming, "For God's sake get up! the ship is going ashore!"

I was so much under the influence of the dream, and assured thereby of Divine protection, that I told him to take my life-preserver, which was hanging up in the cabin, and to save himself. Up he rushed again, life-preserver in hand, while I lay quietly in my berth, listening to all the hubbub and trampling of feet on the deck overhead, until the roar of the breakers and the cessation of blowing off steam, made me rather anxious as to whether I was not, after all, going down. My anxieties soon came to an end. The governor appeared once more, saying all danger was over, and thanked me most warmly for having lent him the life-preserver. It appeared from his rather excited account, that after lifting the anchor to start for Sierra Leone, our next place of call, the rudder-chains got jammed between decks, and the steamer was helplessly drifting ashore. The anchor was then dropped again; but, from some untoward mismanagement, the chain had been detached from the capstan, and slipped through the hawser-holes into the sea, going after the anchor to the bottom.

In this awful predicament we approached the rugged shore, when, at the last moment, the recoil of the heavy seas as they were hurled back into the deep from the shore, jerked the rudder-chains free. The good ship *Harbinger* answered her helm again, and steamed safely away on her mission. The next morning I was congratulated by all on board for my generous conduct in giving my life-preserver to Mr Macdonald (who was rather an elderly personage). So, besides the nuisance of being thanked (which is always a bore), to increase my confusion still more, I knew perfectly well it was utterly undeserved, for I had felt so thoroughly sure of Divine protection when I gave the life-preserver away, that it was evidently useless to me. I never had the courage while on board to tell my dream, through fear of the pitying smiles it would raise; so I passed off, very unwillingly, for a far braver man than I really was.

On arriving at Sierra Leone, some of us landed to visit the garrison and pay our respects to the governor. Colonel O'C——r. The barracks, on the top of the hill overlooking the town, were clean and comfortable; and the officers quite a jolly lot for men stationed in "the white man's grave," as Sierra Leone was then called. The soldiers were smart, well set up, strongly-framed negroes, equal I should say, if well led, to a deal of hard fighting. We found the governor at home, enjoying his pleasant quarters in a private residence, with great equanimity and smiling composure. He was a soft, oily-looking gentleman, considerably yellowed by the fierce glare of the town.

He lay on a couch, decked out with white muslin mosquito-curtains; and gently turning round as we entered, looked like a lump of yellow butter floating in a basin of iced water; and we youngsters were considerably cooled down as we rushed rather heedlessly into the great man's *sanctum sanctorum*. He, however, gracefully ducked his head under the curtains, and waved a ripple of welcome to us all from his extended hands. He was evidently accustomed to unquestioning obedience, so we sat down without saying a word.

The room was full of niggers. It was something wonderful to see them clustered round the bell-shaped muslin curtains of his couch, like busy black flies on a loaf of white crystallised sugar. One had managed to thrust his naked arm, like an antenna, under the folds of the transparent dome, and with a long, white, horse-tail fan, was waving mysterious passes around the yellow, sphinx-shaped head of the presiding deity. Other attendants, with solemn, ebony-wooded heads, were squatting around the place, tossing up and down their lank arms in the most bewildering manner. Now and again they would insert their hands under the arm-pits, then sharply raise them, and with a whack, extend their palms upon the wall. I slipped out of the room, and asked the gallant colonel's orderly the meaning of this mystic performance.

"You see, sir," he said, "those niggers squatting round the room are waiting to relieve the others on duty at the colonel's cot; we makes 'em sit still, for when they goes about they scents mighty strong, and if they sits quite still they gets like rancid cocoa-oil; so to make them as sweet as possible, we orders them to keep alive, pegged down." Poor black wretches! they were writing their misery on the wall, in a manner quite incomprehensible to the gallant colonel.

I next paid a visit to the bishop, who gave me the impression of suffering from a deadly climate, and great despondency as to the prospects of converting the heathen—in fact, he seemed on the point of leaving his flock in this world without the prospect of meeting even one of his black sheep in the next.

In the afternoon Colonel O'C——r returned our visit, and came on board the *Harbinger*. The nimble manner in which he glided up the ladder of the ship, and presented himself in his white toggery to our gasping selves, was a riddle, the solving of which would have melted our brains in that broiling sun. Had it not been for the gleam that shone now and then from his glazed, brown eye, which was like a parched pea, one might have taken him for an automatic mummy. The same horse-tail I mentioned as having been waved over his head while reclining at home, was now carried by himself; and in answer to a question put to him by young K—— of the 74th, he explained that it was a Mandingo emblem of authority, which had the twofold power of keeping off the flies and keeping the niggers in awe. When, in after-life, I became a Turkish *Pasha* with two tails, I often used to look up to the sort of barber's pole on which was appended the same horse-tail token of authority, and think of Colonel O'C——r and the affrighted natives of Sierra Leone.

We now proceeded to St Helena, and visited the residence in which Napoleon died. I was, as we all were, much hurt on finding the neglected state of the building, and of the room in which that great man breathed his last. It was filled with broken agricultural tools and farmyard rubbish; and in the small chamber in which he had described to Montholon how kingdoms were lost and won, cackling poultry were brooding; and that small garden, in which he had spent so many weary hours, trying to dig away the cankering sorrows of his troubled life, was overrun with weeds and scarred with poultry scrabbings.

And so these small, unplastered, half-raftered rooms were the meshes of the net which had held the man-slayer of Europe; and this little plot of ground, scarce larger than a Cockney's flower-bed, all that remained to him who had given realms away! The contrast was too great. There was something that clashed harshly somewhere, and I could not help thinking that posterity would lay this woeful wreck to England's charge.

CHAPTER 3

A Corps of Volunteers Formed

We now proceeded in the same pleasant manner on our way to the Cape, and landed there, after what was then thought a rapid passage of thirty-five days. We found the news from the seat of war was full of the excitement of actual strife, which was being carried on as fiercely as ever. Governor Darling, who appeared to me rather diffident as to his powers of doing good in the colony, with the instructions he had from the Home Government, was nevertheless very active in his efforts to help me. Through his assistance I was enabled, within twenty-four hours of landing, to open an enlisting office. He also stirred up the local authorities and the police to second my efforts. These, and many other kind offices of his, for which I never afterwards had the opportunity of thanking him, I here beg to acknowledge. He is gone now, and I may seem very tardy in expressing my gratitude, but perhaps some of the many who loved him may still listen to my thanks.

Sir Harry Smith, for whom I had letters from the Duke of Wellington, in which, amongst other things, he had kindly said that he *believed me to be a real soldier*—not only had all the resources of Cape Castle and of the commissariat department placed at my disposal, but offered an extra government bounty of two pounds, besides the two offered by me, for every man that enlisted. Poor Sir Harry! Although a fine soldier of the olden class, equal to almost any act of gallantry that required no further intuition than that inspired by actual contact with the foe, he failed during this war for the same reasons that rendered Lord Chelmsford equally unsuccessful during the last, (The Zulu War). The dual character of the local government, it being at the same time civil and military, places serious, almost insurmountable, obstacles, in the way of a commander in the field. On emergencies he is required to consult the wishes and give way to the exigencies of both powers. It would require the capacity and the energy of a Olive or a Stratford to combine, direct, and successfully wield such a power.

In the course of a fortnight upwards of fifty men had joined the corps, and everything promised well for our success; but now difficulties as to the clothing and arming occurred. As the bales were landed from the Harbinger, it was found that the leather jackets for the men had become so shrunk, from the extreme heat in the hold of the ship, that there was no possible means of restoring them to their original shape. The cartridges also had been reduced by water to a mealy pulp, stuck over here and there by pieces of oily white paper like suet in a black pudding. It appeared that the idea of the cartridges being of a highly inflammable nature had pursued the Woolwich authorities so far, that, out of consideration for the safety of the ship and its precious freight, some considerate souls at the dockyard had filled the tin cases, in which the cartridges were packed, *with water*, and then carefully soldered them down.

An enterprising clothier, named Taylour, undertook to make other jackets of a similar nature to those spoiled; and a most intelligent mechanic (a Mr Rawbone, gunsmith of Cape Town) engaged to replace the Minie bullet by another equally effective.

It was an absolute necessity to make another-shaped bullet, as the original Minie was useless without the socket of condensed paper, which I could not procure in the colony. Putting our heads together, we invented a bullet in two unequal sizes, slightly dovetailed together in the centre, and which, under the concussion of lighted gunpowder, were driven into one another, and thus expanding, filled up the grooves of the rifle, took the twist, and went spinning through the air on its axis, as true in its flight as the Minie. I was also greatly aided by a Mr Andersen, a Norwegian gentleman, an enthusiastic sportsman and traveller, at the Cape. He took an almost passionate interest in me, my task, and the Minie rifle. From him I gained much useful information concerning bush-life, and the habits, history, and traditions of the *Kaffir* tribes. He had very little faith in the half-worldly, half-sentimental policy of the British Government towards the *Kaffir* and the Dutch settler; and my experience afterwards only confirmed the truth of his observations.

I now began to practise the men with their firelocks. As this was almost the only drilling they got, there remained plenty of spare time for drinking-bouts in public-houses, and for them to spend their bounty-money and report on the glorious advantages of being *soldiers in prospective*.

I had, amongst the men, enlisted a noted character at Cape Town called "Happy Jack." Evans was his real name, a common sailor now, but who had been boatswain in the navy.

He was rarely in barracks, but always to be hailed, as he good-naturedly explained to the guard on duty, in such or such a public-house. It may be readily supposed that men enlisted under the auspices of Happy Jack were not the best of characters; in fact, many of them were what they termed at the Cape, *laggers*— that is to say, men who, having got away from Norfolk Island, or other penfolds for black sheep, lag behind, under guardianship of Dutch laws at the Cape, instead of trusting their precious selves to the supervision of their own natural police at home.

The local authorities, however, with the praiseworthy object of dispersing the scabby flock under their charge, provided the ranks of my corps with some desperate cases, whom they ordered to enlist as the alternative of going to prison. I had a shrewd guess as to the meaning of these energetic efforts to strengthen the force under my command; but I used to shut my eyes as closely as possible in accepting the proffered services of some of my recruits, and unless something too glaring forced itself on my attention—such as a man with one arm, a wooden leg, or stone blind—I used to accept the services of almost all, and place them at Her Majesty's disposal,—taking often, when tempted, a cripple, as the necessary evil attendant upon the services of a good man, these being the conditions on which the contract was several times concluded between myself and the police.

No doubt I was often undecided as to whether or not I should attempt to knock down the authors of some of the practical jokes that were played upon me; but when I came to reflect that my best friends at the Cape advised me strongly to go home and leave the *Kaffirs* alone, I could not feel much surprised that stupid people, to whom I was unknown, should be much more practical in their method of enforcing the same opinion upon me.

And truly my position seemed a riddle in more ways than one. I was very young—scarcely twenty-two, and looked still younger. I was spending large sums at the Cape to regain a footing in the British army, when I might have easily purchased, for a tenth of the money, a commission at home. My ways were foreign. I had been brought up mostly abroad—in France and Germany. My military notions were based on their schools. My actual experience of war had been gained in Algeria, Hungary, and in the streets of Paris and Vienna during the late revolutions, where I had taken somewhat more than a strict observer's part on the side of legal authority.

I could not understand the half-military, half-civilian existence of a British officer, and, excepting the Artillery and Engineers, thought them a very unscientific lot. No one could doubt their fighting capacity; but their capabilities for undertaking a campaign against European armies was very dubious in my sight.

An enthusiast myself in my belief in Christ, I yet belonged to no Church in Christendom—in short, I have often wondered since how I escaped shipwreck amidst the shoals and breakers that surrounded me.

Two bright spots alone shone through this turmoil and anxiety. At the Cape, Colonel Neville Chamberlain and Major Quinn (two nobler specimens of the conquerors of India could hardly be found) took me kindly by the hand; and as they told me, how with quiet demeanour and ironside determination of will, native levies were led, and victories won in India, I humbly resolved to follow, if I could, the noble example they gave me. An anecdote concerning a sword which Colonel Neville Chamberlain presented me with, may not be out of place in these pages. It was a weapon that had fallen into his hands after an engagement, and was considered a splendid specimen of Indian workmanship.

In the year 1853 I was sent on a mission to Constantinople, and took the sword with me, and used to wear it in my frequent visits to the Seraskierat. Riza Pasha, who then presided there, asked me one day to allow him to look at it, and after gravely reading the Arabic characters embossed upon the blade, passed it on to other members of the council board. One and all seemed much surprised at the writing, and at my being the possessor of such a weapon. Mr Sarel, the dragoman of the embassy, who was with me at the time, explained how it came from India, and into my possession. Riza asked to be allowed to show it to the *Sultan*, to which I consented, but never could get it returned.

As, however, I repeatedly asked for it, and threatened to speak to the ambassador on the subject, Riza one day sent me another sword, with a firman in a white satin bag, containing my nomination to the colonelcy of the second regiment of the *Sultan's* Roumelian Guard. I was rather induced to look upon the affair as a mystification; but Sarel explained to me that it was quite serious, and in reality a compliment paid to Lord Stratford de Redcliffe, and that I had better accept the sword and the commission, as I should never see Colonel Chamberlain's sword again. In this manner I entered the Turkish army; and although I never assumed the actual command as colonel, it was (by a strange coincidence) one of those regiments that formed the brigade of cavalry which I afterwards commanded on the Danube.

It was a curiously-officered regiment. I, the colonel, had been named through being the possessor of a certain sword; the lieutenant-colonel. Said Bey, through being the possessor of a wonderful flute (he had been chief flute-player to the *Sultan*); one of the majors, Mourad Bey, for being a renegade Frenchman; and the other major, an Irishman, for being the supposed son of an English Prime Minister. The men, however, were splendid fellows, and some became passionately attached to me.

As a proof of this, one day when, as quartermaster-general of the Turkish forces, I was sending to Eupatoria, in the Crimea, Osman Pasha's army from Cisebole, in the Bay of Bourgas, Halil Pasha, brother-in-law of the *Sultan*, and commander of the Turkish cavalry, refused to obey my repeated orders concerning the embarkation of the women of his *harem* (a proceeding to which I was opposed), when, at my command, two of my orderlies—Mourad and Mahamet-Chousch—took him by the "scruff" of the neck, before the whole of his staff, and pitched him off the pier into the sea, after his screaming women.

Not a man stirred an inch to save him until I gave orders to do so; and the half-drowned *Pasha* contented himself with writing a long letter of complaint to Lord Stratford de Redcliffe, who, in reply, said he only got what he deserved.

CHAPTER 4

Prepare to Start for the Front

To return to my men at the Cape;—Happy Jack and I, after many a good look at one another, were gradually nearing the point of trying conclusions as to which of the two really commanded the corps. On his part it was one perpetual scene of half-drunken, half-intentional defiance. He rolled about the streets in uniform, followed by besotted comrades, to gain, as he said, by their jolly appearance, fresh adherents. No one, he pretended, could look at their happy condition and refuse to join such companions. The fact is, he did bring in many recruits, and I hardly knew how to get on with or without him. Providence, however, decided in my favour. Colonel Ingleby, commandant of the town and castle, a fine old soldier, and extremely kind to me, sent a small detachment of artillerymen to keep order in the barracks.

Happy Jack's fate was sealed. A picket of regulars sent to scour the public-houses for absentees, brought Jack to barracks in a woeful plight. He had had a frog's march—that is to say, on hands, belly, and knees—almost from one end of the town to the other. Refusing to obey the picket, and march to barracks on his legs, he had been kindly allowed to come on all-fours, held up by the collar of his coat, for fear of stumbling, and the seat of his unmentionables. Poor fellow! he felt sorely his abject degradation in the eyes of his associates, male and female, and kept ever afterwards well in the background.

The day now approached for our starting to the front. Captain Hall, who commanded the man-of-war on the station, had prepared to take us all on board, but the difficulty was how to get the men there. Everyone knew perfectly well, from their many loud boastings on the point, that they had not the least intention of going; and as no means existed in the town by which forcible coercion could be attempted on so large a body of men with a reasonable chance of success, it did look a very dubious question.

The matter, however, was finally arranged after this fashion, between Captain Hall, Colonel Ingleby, the police, and myself. We were to have a grand field-day, to end by a display of military prowess on the part of the men in a sham engagement, and thereby prove their fighting capacity against Her Majesty's sable foes. The general plan consisted in the police, and all the artillerymen Colonel Ingleby could spare, landing on the beach just outside the castle, under the protection of the guns of Captain Hall's ship. They were then to proceed inland towards Wineberg, and, on arriving about two miles from the shore, were to be suddenly confronted by my corps, and driven back to the ship. The first part of the plan was carried out as intended. In the first place, Colonel Ingleby, in full uniform, attended by a sub-lieutenant, Dr B——, and two commissariat officers in regimentals, passed a review of the men, 167 rank and file. They looked very well in line, and knew enough drill to take open order for inspection; so that the first part of the programme gave every appearance of having a happy issue, by the way in which it was being carried out.

Colonel Ingleby, however, had the unfortunate idea to make the men a speech in praise of their gallant appearance. This was not in the order-book, so I scarcely knew what to say in reply. Happy Jack, however, was equal to the occasion. He stepped boldly out of the ranks and walked up to the colonel, and said that as he was so pleased with their trim, he hoped he would, man-o'-war fashion, order a glass of grog all round. The good-tempered colonel, rather taken aback, replied, "You had better ask Captain Lakeman for that." "No, no," said Jack; "I know better than to ask the skipper when the admiral is present, so please order the grog." It *was* ordered. The colonel drank to our success, I returned thanks, the men cheered, and then broke out with "We won't go home till morning."

In the course of half an hour passed in this agreeable manner, the men fell readily enough into the ranks, and proceeded in a rollicking, spirited manner towards the position assigned us in the forthcoming engagement. We had hardly taken up our post in the bend of the road that led to the Observatory, when the continued booming of Captain Hall's guns told us the enemy were disembarking. Shortly afterwards they could be espied feeling their way through the brushwood that led up the valley. In approaching the cross-road that wound its way towards Wineberg they divided their forces.

One party—the police—took the road; the other—the regulars—continued their way through the scrubby brushwood. They advanced but slowly, taking all due precautions, probing the ground right and left, with an advance and a rear guard. The police, on the contrary, came up the dusty road in a most disorderly, unhesitating manner—looking like a swarm of bluebottles on a white, smoking, Cambridge sausage. This was setting such a bad example to my recruits that I determined to give them a profitable lesson; so, calling in the outposts, I prepared to meet them suddenly with the whole force at my disposal.

On they heedlessly came to the bend of the road, when they found themselves confronted by an impassable barrier of prickly cactus, that I had hastily strewn there. They evidently thought this a warning of approaching danger, for, hastily unslinging their carbines, they prepared for action. But I left them no time for this ceremonious proceeding. The order to fire was given, and these brave but misguided invaders received such a peppering discharge from both sides of the road that the error of their ways became pungently manifest; and, without the slightest demur, they wriggled their bent forms into the smallest possible shape, and bolted in the opposite direction.

But my men were most anxious to prove their capacity for far harder fighting than the evanescent police force allowed them to display; so, with loud shouts and exulting halloos, they jumped up from behind the fence which had hitherto concealed them, and started off in pursuit of the scuttling foe.

Many a long itching grudge was feelingly rubbed off that day upon the heads of the police. Happy Jack was particularly conspicuous, as, with tucked-up sleeves, he laid the butt of his rifle (much to my dread of its breaking) upon the heads and shoulders of his natural enemies, in a manner quite uncalled for by the stricken.

But there is a turn in the tide of events which, taken at the flood, makes one at times feel somewhat giddy as it whirls us round. This dizzying ebb of fortune ran counter to Happy Jack, and threw him on his beam-ends in the most reckless fashion.

It happened that Sergeant Herridge of the police force, and in command of that party, seeing the discomfiture of his men, had had the discretion to lead them back to Cape Town, and was showing the way as fast as his portly person, under the swelter-ing heat of the sun and the battle combined, allowed him to do. Happy Jack espied the retreating chief, and took up the pursuit like Achilles after affrighted Hector, chivvying him round and round his admiring followers.

At length he reached the spent chieftain, and placing the muz-zle of his firelock between the outspread coat-tails of the flying victim, blew a cartridge off at that part upon which people usu-ally sit. The effect was startling. Hector cut a double-shuffle high up in the air like an exploding cracker, and while still wreathed in smoke, swung round his truncheon with Parthian address on the grinning face of Jack, whose head came to the ground— cracker number two.

Now was the time for the victorious sergeant to make off: the road was clear, and he had my good wishes that it should be kept so. But the foolish fellow, instead of running away, to live and fight another day, sat deliberately down in the dusty road and began bumping his hindquarters violently on the ground, to stamp out the fire the cartridge of Happy Jack had lit in his rear.

This ludicrous display of stern-firing gave time for other men to come up; he was made prisoner, and Jack, recovering his senses, feelingly kicked the fire out of the singeing sergeant in double-quick time. Herridge was removed on board in a critical state, refusing in his disgraced condition to be taken to Cape Town; ultimately, upon recovery, he enlisted in my corps.

On the discomfiture of the police, the artillerymen in the valley began to retreat; but in this direction the pursuit was very slack. My men bent all their energies in scattering every vestige of civil authority; they evidently began to consider themselves as one with the soldiers—in fact, it was in recounting the mishaps that had that day befallen the police that we retired laughingly together, with those whom we were supposed to be repulsing with great vigour.

Finally, on arriving at the beach from whence the enemy had started, a still greater surprise awaited us; but this time (as if by just reprisal) it fell exclusively upon my own men, and that in a most bewildering manner.

Captain Hall had landed his marines and a detachment of blue-jackets, who, *sans cérémonie*, disarmed my men, as they arrived in batches of twos and threes, and placed them in files along the sea-shore. The climax had arrived; and to the astonishment, no doubt, of many beholders from the town, who had come to witness what they supposed was likely to be an exciting performance, I was quite equal to the task of stage-manager on this occasion. In a few words I explained to my future heroes that the time was come to go to the front and show to the *Kaffirs* what we were capable of doing. The black was pressing hard on the white man, who looked to us for help; the ship was ready to convey us; the cheers of the inhabitants of Cape Town were a token of what was expected; in fact, the time had arrived when the very humblest had a duty to perform. Go we must; so I called for three cheers, and "Forward to the boats!"

Some murmured that they had not wished friends "good-bye;" others talked of kits left behind; but they were too tired to resist physically, and without consultation they were unequal to combined action; so, *nolens volens*, we managed, one after another, to get them all aboard ship, excepting some twenty or so, who had come to grief in our late engagement with the police, and these I left behind. By the exertions of Captain Hall, who appeared to me a most painstaking, energetic officer, we soon got safely stowed away on board, and three days after landed at Port Elizabeth. Mr Durant Deare, a merchant of that town, kindly offered me quarters under his hospitable roof. The men were billeted in the town; and two days afterwards, with seven waggon-loads of ammunition and five gun-carriages, we started for Graham's Town.

Foreseeing the disorderly manner in which my rough lot would probably leave the grog-shops, I started very early in the morning, before the inhabitants had got up—for I was loath to show our, as yet, disorganised state. I waited until fairly on the march before bringing a tighter hand to bear upon the many ruffians in my corps, who, half in joke, half inquiringly, looked me in the face, and called me mate, skipper, or captain, as they interpreted its meaning.

On the evening of the second day we arrived at the Ada bush; this was some twenty miles in breadth, composed of jungle-wood, free from *Kaffirs*, but infested with bands of marauders, consisting of native levies who had fled, weapons in hand, from the seat of war. As we were encamped that night, I strolled the greater part of it around the fires, and gathered from several parties that the next day something eventful was to take place in which my fate was concerned. I felt perfectly tranquil, however, trusting that I should be equal to the task of holding my own against such an abandoned, disunited lot—for I had also many good, God-fearing men among them.

The next morning, on the order being given for the men to fall in for roll-call, no one stirred. Sergeant Waine, who had been a non-commissioned officer in the 44th, but broken and discharged for bad conduct, to whom I had given the stripes in consideration of his regimental knowledge, stepped up to me, and said that the men wanted grog served out to them before they would budge, and if they did not get it, would return to Port Elizabeth. I did not reply to him, but, getting on my horse, rode up to the men and asked if they had enlisted with the intention of obeying orders or not. No one replied; and giving the word to fall in, they sullenly did so.

The Hottentot drivers *inspanned* the bullocks, and I repeated "Forward!" in a tone that seemed strange even to myself, so authoritative and full of energy did it sound in my own ear. All obeyed, and we started on the march; scarcely, however, had we entered the bush before a shot was fired. I saw from the smoke where the discharge came from, so, riding to the spot, inquired who had fired. Sergeant Waine came to the front and said he had. I reminded him of the order which had been given that no firing was to take place under any consideration, unless I or Lieutenant Pilkington gave the command.

He muttered something unintelligible in reply; and I repeated the order aloud, to be heard by all around, that if any man discharged a firelock without orders I would have him punished as severely as the circumstances allowed. I then rode on again towards the head of the column, when another shot was fired, and this time the bullet came whistling very close to my head. On looking round I saw that the shot was fired from the same spot again, around which the men were now gathered in a cluster. I felt that the crisis had come, so loosening my pistol in the holster-pipe (an Adams' revolver, one of the first made), I rode back and asked who fired. Waine replied he did.

"Who gave the order?" said I.

"A magpie," he answered.

I called out for Sergeant-Major Herridge, the late police officer, who had quite recovered, and had become a most efficient subordinate. "Take Waine's firelock from him," I said. This was quickly done. "Now tie him up to that gun-carriage and give him three dozen." Waine bawled out to the men, and asked whether they would see him flogged like a nigger. Before they could reply I drove my horse amidst them, revolver in hand, and cried out that the first man who opened his mouth, or moved, I

29

would blow his brains out, at the same time pointing the muzzle to some of their heads, as I saw they were more or less inclined to disobey my injunctions.

Sergeant Herridge was a powerful man, and Waine was soon tied up; but there being no "cat" to flog him with, I ordered it to be done with his belt. And well was it laid on. The fellow bellowed lustily, and I asked the men what they thought of such a blubbering cur. Happy Jack now began to cry "Shame." I rode him down, and as he scrambled from between my horse's legs in an awful state of funk, some of the men laughed outright, and he got no more openly-shown sympathy than his comrade Waine. After the flogging was over I told Herridge to give back to Waine his leather jacket.

The ruffian said, "You will give me my jacket, but why don't you give me my firelock?"

"Give him that also," said I. On getting it he began loading, and looking at me in a most significant manner. When he came to put the cap on the nipple, either from the numbing pain of the flogging, or from the violence with which Herridge had pulled off his pouch, he could not find a cap. I offered him one—it was only a pistol cap (but I did not think of that at the time); when he looked at me, threw down his firelock, and said, "No, I won't shoot you." Seeing this sign in my favour, I began to explain to the men that no one had a greater horror, of flogging than I had, and that I never would have had it done had it not been to punish a cowardly villain who had attempted to shoot me from behind. If any of them had a complaint to make, let them come to me, face to face, and explain, and they never would find me unwilling to listen, or to redress any just grievance. Waine was then placed on a gun-carriage alongside of Happy Jack, and we once more started on our march. From that day my orders were obeyed, and matters assumed a more orderly aspect.

On fording Sunday River, which runs through the Ada bush, the whole column nearly came to grief. All due precautions had, however, been taken as though passing through an enemy's country, lining both sides of the ford—an advanced-guard and a rear-guard. But notwithstanding orders, some of the men had strolled down the banks of the river in order to find a favourable spot to bathe. While thus proceeding, some marauding *Fingoes* were espied; a cry arose that the *Kaffirs* were coming, a stampede ensued, and my men bolted like rabbits into the bush. The Hottentot drivers cut the traces of their oxen, disappearing with their cattle, and I was left alone with the waggons in the middle of the river, with five or six men whom I had managed to keep together—my anxiety barely sufficing to retain my laughter at the ridiculous disappearance of the whole party.

The *Fingoes*, however, were as much frightened as my men had been, and ran away in the opposite direction; so when my fellows had been sufficiently scratched and blown by making their way through the prickly under-wood, unmolested by all except their own fears (and the thorns), they soon retraced their foot-steps, and could be seen in twos and threes peeping from the outskirts of the jungle to know whether the coast had become clear. On getting them together again, I made a speech, and so enlarged upon their ridiculously discreditable behaviour, that they swore, one and all, that they would never so commit themselves again. To put their courage to the test, I determined to encamp that night where this occurred—in the middle of the bush. This was rather hazardous; but I counted upon the danger of *Fingo* marauders to keep them together, and in my own bold attitude to keep the latter off.

My position was a strange one; and as I lay that night upon a gun-carriage, having for companions Waine moaning over the pains in his back, and Happy Jack muttering threats of courts-martial, I thought, if Providence did not intervene, the thread of my existence would possibly snap somehow.

The night passed off calmly enough, and the next morning saw us safely on the other side of the bush; and that evening we encamped at a farm belonging to Mr Bruckyer, a Dutch settler from Haarlem—which town, by the way, was the home of my forefathers in King William III.'s reign; therefore, being somewhat akin through ancestral associations, we soon became good friends. This gentleman not only furnished my corps with an abundance of farm produce—accepting only our thanks in return—but also took charge of seven men who were incapable, from illness and sore feet, of continuing with the column. These men were afterwards sent on in a waggon to Fort Beaufort, some hundred and twenty miles off, to rejoin the corps. Mr Bruckyer again refused all remuneration.

CHAPTER 5

March into Graham's Town

As a rule, I found the settlers—English and Dutch—a fine, generous-hearted set of people; and many of them who read these lines may, I hope, think with pleasure of the happy times we passed together.

It was a great relief to get rid of my sick men, as I had no medical man with the corps; and the only medicines or pharmaceutical knowledge I possessed were gleaned from a small medicine-chest I had purchased at Port Elizabeth. It was one of the ceaseless threats of Happy Jack that I had had a man flogged without a medical man being present, and without having remedies at hand in case of accident.

The next day we proceeded to Mr Judd's farm, some ten miles farther on the road. Here I had an opportunity of showing what the Minie rifle could perform. We were sitting under the veranda of Mr Judd's house examining one of the men's rifles, and I was explaining the advantage of a rapid twist with an elongated bullet having an expansive base, &c. Mr Judd asked if it would reach some bullocks which were grazing five or six hundred yards off, adding that I might try if I liked, for the cattle were his. To this I consented; and laying the rifle on the balcony as a rest, I singled out a bullock to his attention—fired. I had the satisfaction that, either from the whistling of the ball or from being actually struck, the mark had been attained, for the animal immediately started off at a trot.

All doubts, however, soon came to an end; for the poor brute lay down, and before we could reach the spot, had died,—the ball had passed through its body. This, no doubt, was a great fluke; but it had the good result of proving the value of the weapon to the men (a great many were looking on while I fired), and also leading them to suppose I was a first-rate shot.

At this farm I also had the satisfaction of getting rid of Happy Jack. I afforded him the opportunity of deserting during the night, which he availed himself of; and I took particular care not to have him awakened the next morning as we departed, although I knew he was lying drunk in a cattle-*kraal* a short way off. Waine became much more humble after Jack's desertion, and before we reached Graham's Town had been restored to the ranks. So all fear of my being called up before a court-martial for flogging a man with an illegal instrument—which his belt undoubtedly was—soon disappeared.

We made a great sensation on our entrance into Graham's Town: the gun-carriages, wrapped up in hay to prevent any ill effects from the heat of the sun, might be readily taken for real artillery. The men—mostly seafaring people, with big rounded shoulders, bronzed faces, and long hirsute appendages—might, for size and determination of look, compare advantageously with any troops in the colony. They also wore leather helmets somewhat similar to those now adopted in the service, which added considerably to their martial appearance; and altogether they presented to the beholder (who knew nothing of their bolting proclivities, as lately displayed in the Ada bush) a most formidable accession to Her Majesty's forces at the Cape.

It may not be out of place to give a slight outline of the officers who commanded my detachment.

My first lieutenant, ——, a near relative of Lord ——'s, was a tall, handsome fellow, who had been in Her Majesty's service, of rather loose habits; not wanting in pluck, but fonder of excitement over the card-table than in the field.

My second lieutenant was named H——d, an enthusiast on the mission of Christianity. He had been lately suffering from brain fever, and with his hair cropped short, tall, gaunt figure, and deep-set, glistening eyes, looked the modern representative of one of Cromwell's Ironsides. In spirit, he was a man all over; and had he possessed more *physique* to ballast his mental faculties, would have left no inconsiderable mark in this world. As I pen these lines, I feel he was *un grand homme manqué*, and regret that a word I spoke during the heat of an engagement, and which he misinterpreted, caused him to resign.

My third lieutenant, named P——n, was a gentleman by birth, and had been in Her Majesty's service, but had advisedly resigned after having thrown a glass of wine in his superior officer's face. He was of a tall, lusty figure, full of animal courage, and fond of animal enjoyment.

Sergeant-Major Herridge I have already described.

Sergeant Beaufort had been in the Rifle Brigade: he was the handsomest man I perhaps ever beheld; with short, crisp, light chestnut locks, full, oval countenance, tall stature—six feet two inches—and well-rounded limbs. He looked the picture of what Richard Coeur de Lion might have been.

Sergeant Shelley had been in the 60th Rifles: a tall, lank fellow, with arms and legs on the move, like a windmill in a gale of wind—always threatening to fly off at a tangent, but nevertheless fixed to his post. He became very attached to me; and many a time, while thinking myself alone in the bush, Sergeant Shelley would appear at my side, with "All right, captain; here I am;" and all right it was, for the man was a host in himself, through his acuteness, strength, and daring.

Another character was Sergeant Dix. He had been a well-to-do confectioner in Cape Town, who had left pastry and the sweets of marriage life to join my corps, owing, it was surmised, to the depredations of an officer on the presiding goddess of his wedding-cake. Poor Dix! he used to make the men suffer to ease his own pains. Up and down the lines he used to *fizz* with his fat podgy legs, basting the men with the hot drippings of his marital wrath, until at last I was obliged to reduce him to the ranks, and install him as *chef* in my own cuisine. Such is a faint outline of the corps which I marched through the town, and encamped some three miles on the other side, owing to my well-founded dread of the grog-shops.

It was here that I first became acquainted with the shortcomings of the service.

Colonel Cloëte, the quartermaster-general, had no more idea as to the ammunition I had brought from Port Elizabeth than what he had to do with it. He knew, certainly, what requisitions he had received, but he knew no more than I did what reserves, not actually wanted, existed in those places. The waggons that brought the ammunition, and had given me such anxiety on the road, were left, during my ten days' stay in Graham's Town, in the open streets; not a sentry or guard of any sort—the Hottentot drivers, with pipes in their mouths, seeming the presiding guardians over British military stores.

The commissariat was in the hands of the tradesmen of the town: a Mr J———s (banker and merchant) seemed to have the whole charge of the provisioning of the army. He was exceedingly kind and courteous, a perfect gentleman in all his doings, but yet not the right person in the right place, I thought. Of the military stragglers in the town, they were the usual rag-tag and bobtail lot always to be found compassing the rear of an army actively engaged in the field.

After waiting twelve days, I at last received orders to proceed to Fort Beaufort. The men being in fair condition by this time, I determined to cover the distance (about forty miles) in two days. This was easily accomplished; and rather to the surprise of the commander-in-chief, I presented myself at headquarters.

CHAPTER 6

In Action

I gave a report in writing of my doings on the road, and my estimation of the resources and failings as a military road, that it professed. Amongst other things, I stated the fact of seeing a strong detachment of the 12th Regiment uselessly guarding a fort of no possible influence in the actual state of the war. This brought the staff down upon me; but I was thanked by the general, who, as a token of welcome, presented me with a fine chestnut charger.

The next day I was perfectly astounded at the close proximity of the *Kaffirs*. There they were in shoals, perfectly unmolested, on the slopes of the Waterkloof, and within twelve miles of thousands of British troops. I had seen on many occasions the daring indifference of the Kabyles of the Atlas Mountains, but that was displayed on chance occasions; but here a badly-armed, undisciplined throng of naked savages braved with impunity, day after day, week after week, the energies of the British empire. I was utterly staggered for a moment by such a display, but was not long in volunteering to make a closer acquaintance with these sable heroes and their strongholds. I, however, received a good snubbing for my pains.

At last a grand expedition was planned, under General Napier, to attack this said Waterkloof, and my corps was assigned the post of advanced-guard. The first day we reached Blink water Post, where I made the acquaintance of the commander, W——d; he appeared to me one of the right sort, although rather uselessly employed. This is one of the great faults of our service, to place a brilliant, dashing officer to guard an exposed, permanent position, when a good, stolid, ordinary-being would have done quite as well, if not better. The art of war is like the game of chess, and I would not give much for the guiding hand that does not know the value and place of each figure on the board.

The next day, after a somewhat tiring ascent, we crowned the heights of the Waterkloof, without firing a shot or seeing many *Kaffirs*. I was then ordered to attack the Horse-shoe—a half-circular line of bush that fringed the precipitous heights. This was a difficult task, from the formation of the ground and the disheartening reminiscences, it was murmured, which were attached to the spot. Here it was that Colonel Fordyce had been lately killed, and the 74th fearfully handled. The Honourable R C——, the staff officer who ordered the movement, pointed in a somewhat vague manner to the centre of the half-moon as the place on which I was to begin the attack.

This undefined indication left me a considerable margin; so I managed, in the mile of ground I had to cover before coming within range of the *Kaffir* guns, to oblique so much to the right, that I came very near that end of the Horse-shoe. As I got within range, my men being in very loose order (this being their first engagement, there was naturally some hesitation and wavering along the line), a shot fired by some good marksman on the enemy's side, brought my orderly, David McIntyre, to the ground with a ball through the chest.

The whole line stopped as if struck by an electric shock. Another shot as effective as the last would, I felt sure, send them to the right-about; so I ran to the front and shouted out, "We shall all be shot if we remain here in the open! To the bush, my lads! to the bush!"

The sense of this order was obvious. We shouted "Hurrah!" as much to drown our own fears as to frighten the enemy; and amidst a rattling fire, more noisy than dangerous, we, for safety's sake, gallantly charged the foe. The *Kaffirs* and Hottentots were evidently taken by surprise at this display of gallantry—latterly all the charges had been on their side. The tables were turned, and instead of red-jackets, it was for black-skins to fall back.

Once in the bush, what with cheering and firing, we kept up such a hullabaloo, that the niggers must have thought all the white devils of Christendom were let loose upon them. I, who knew where the row came from, was astonished at the effect upon my own nerves, as the adjoining rocks reverberated the sound of our advance. We literally chased the foe like rabbits through the bush, and came out at the other end of the Horse-shoe, rather disappointed than otherwise in not meeting with more resistance. We then fell back on the main body, having performed our task with a decided dash and very slight loss—two killed and five wounded.

As we were quite unmolested by the foe, it was admirable to see the cool, collected manner in which my men retired—in fact, I was not at all astonished when General Napier sent a staff officer to thank us for our gallant and orderly bearing. We now proceeded to breakfast, and had hardly begun, when the same officer came back and told me to advance with my men and endeavour to dislodge the *Kaffirs* from some rough boulders of rock on the edge of the *kloof*, some two miles on our left. Now this order was unadvisable for many reasons: from the lie of the ground it had no strategical importance; it neither threatened the enemy's stronghold, nor in any way interfered with movements we might make to carry it.

My men had had a long march, which, combined with the efforts in clearing out the Horse-shoe, had left us without any physical energy; whilst there were whole battalions who had not fired a shot, and were eager for an opportunity to distinguish themselves.

I, however, kept these reasonings to myself; and giving the men orders to prepare for action, they sprang to their feet with far more alacrity than I had a right to expect.

In going to take up the ground assigned to us as the point of attack, we passed in front of the main body, and the general came up and shook hands with me. This cheering token sent us on in good spirits to within about a thousand yards of the rocks above named. I here sent a small detachment down a slope of ground that led somewhat to our left, to threaten, if possible, the flank and rear of the position in our front.

With the rest of the men I obliqued slightly to the right, with the same object of turning the rear in that direction also.

We had advanced about half-way when the guns of Captain Rowley's battery opened fire over our heads. This caused considerable uneasiness; the men were not accustomed to the hurling noise rushing over their heads from the rear: some ducked, some stopped, others went on; and the line, which hitherto had been so well kept, assumed a most zigzag, mob-looking appearance.

I have often observed that even veterans waver and become confused under this meteor-discharge overhead. The *Kaffirs*, however, did not seem to be much frightened by the shot or the shell. They fielded for the cannon-shot as they rebounded from the rocks as though they were cricket-balls. These same balls were much prized as pestles for grinding purposes.

As for the shells, they no sooner burst than, in derision, the *Kaffirs* picked pieces up and pretended to throw them back at us. But now a rocket that was intended to astonish the *Kaffirs* came so close over us, that the whole line started and ducked their heads in the most ridiculous fashion. This profound *salaam*, as we faced the foe, elicited from them a tremendous shout of approval in return. I profited by this humility of ours, and as my fellows had their faces so close to the ground, I ordered them to lie down altogether. "Raise the sighting on the rifles for six hundred yards. Take steady aim. Fire!"

At the first discharge the *Kaffirs* scuttled from the rocks in flying order, leaving, however, several of their bodies on the ground. So the Minie rifle did in one minute what six guns and rocket-tubes had been attempting for the last quarter of an hour.

In the course of five minutes' firing not a *Kaffir* was to be seen; even the wounded who lay on the ground were left quite uncared for; and what was far dearer still to a *Kaffir's* heart, blankets and *karosses* were also left behind.

I then cautiously advanced to within a short distance of the rocks. The men lay down once more, to wait for the flanking party to begin on our left; but they had gone too far down, and when at length they began firing, it had no influence on the *Kaffirs* behind the rocks facing us. It was difficult now to know what to do. The enemy was far too strong for us to carry the position by a front attack, and my flanking party seemed, by the sound of the firing, to be rather going from than approaching us. At this critical moment the recall sounded far away in the rear, and never sound struck my ear more cheerfully before. We fell back in the most orderly manner; and the *Kaffirs*, coming out in great numbers from behind the rocks to survey our retreat, received a last volley in return, which quickly sent them to the right-about.

The Minie rifle taught them this day a lesson which they ever after identified with my men, and they never forgot its instructive teaching. We were now sent to take up our quarters near the spot where the attack had commenced in the morning. We were to remain there until further orders. A body of the regular forces was also sent to take up a position about a mile in the rear; while the main body marched back again to headquarters at Fort Beaufort.

I immediately set to work, throwing up a defence against a night attack; and before evening set in—there being an abundance of stone material at hand—I had thrown up a tolerably strong defence. The next day was the first at which I assisted at public prayers in the colony. My men and I were perched on the huge boulders of rock that fringe the Waterkloof height, and from the depths below arose, in childlike strains, the glorious morning hymn—

Awake, my soul, and with the sun
Thy daily course of duty run.

These sable children were awakening their souls to their daily duty of cutting white men's throats. Something like awe crept over me at this Heaven-beseeching. It was one of those mysterious results of missionary instruction of which I do not profess to know the ABC; it was giving to this would-be slayer the name of fratricide. I got up in a hurry and left the spot.

This awakening of Cain made me feel very much as Abel must have felt had he been able to run away. But these poor Hottentots, with a strong predilection for settling disputes with their white brother, after the antediluvian fashion of knocking you upon the head with a *knobkerrie*, were still much to be pitied, taken as they were from their boundless homes and pent up in that wooded vale below, singing of their freedom in Christ, like caged mocking-birds imitating the hollow sound of words that convey soul-stirring thoughts to man. I felt more sympathy for them than for those who had brought them to that state.

In the course of a few days I had raised a barricade round my camp strong enough to resist any number of *Kaffirs*; and having thus secured a good base of operation, began to look about me as to how I could best make use of it for offensive movements.

Colonel N——, the officer who commanded the regulars left on the heights, did not at this time interfere in any manner with my proceedings, so I was left perfectly free, and decided that, with the small body of men at my disposal, night attacks were the only reasonable operations to be undertaken with any hope of permanent success. The *Kaffir*, lithe, supple, and vicious as a snake during the heat of the day, loses much of his treacherous energy at night. Ignorant and superstitious, he would be already half conquered by further increasing his dread of darkness; while the white man during the refreshing coolness of night was at his best at the Cape; and bugle-sounds allowed him to be governed almost as easily as during the day. I accordingly proceeded cautiously to accustom the men to the work. We now received in camp a copy of a general order thus worded:—

Headquarters, Fort Beaufort.
General Napier speaks in the highest terms of the discernment and gallantry displayed by Captain Lakeman, and the

bravery and good conduct of his men on this their first engagement with the enemy.

(Signed)   A. J. Cloëte,

Quartermaster-General.

This was very gratifying, and we determined to obtain still further recognitions of services rendered. In the course of a month we had so far created a panic by our night attacks, that the *Kaffirs* evacuated the whole of the table-land surrounding the Waterkloof, and retired to the valley and rocky recesses below.

CHAPTER 7

Night Fighting

Another attack on a still grander scale than the last was now decided on at headquarters; and the commander-in-chief, General Cathcart, with several thousand troops, guns, &c., were accordingly assembled on the heights overlooking the *kloof*. It was, however, a somewhat tame affair. We merely marched round the heights, and only attacked a small *Kaffir* village on the edge of a promontory, called Mundell's Peak, that advanced like a wedge into the middle of the above-named *kloof* and almost divided it in two.

This operation fell to my share, and was, I think, effectually done in fair military style. In the general orders issued relating to the events of the day, it stated:—

> In the attack and carrying of Mundell's Peak, the gallantry and spirited conduct of Lakeman's corps and its commander, it is gratifying to the Commander of the Forces to take this opportunity to notice.
>
> (Signed)   A. J. Cloëte,
>   Quartermaster-General

During this day I observed a tenacity of life which seemed incredible. A soldier of the Rifle Brigade, in looking over the edge of the *kloof*, was shot through the head. I was on horseback close to him at the time; I dismounted, propped him up with his pack, picked up the cap which had been knocked off by the shot, and placed it with my handkerchief over his face. The body was shortly afterwards put on a stretcher and taken to Post Reteif, several miles off, then commanded by Captain Bruce (King Bruce they called him), a gallant and hospitable soldier. On the evening of the same day I saw the man there, still breathing, with a hole in his head through which you might have passed a ramrod, and he only died towards the next morning.

After this imposing parade of troops, the main force marched back again to Fort Beaufort; but the commander-in-chief decided that two forts were to be constructed on the heights, about a mile to the rear of where I was stationed. Colonel ——, R. E., was intrusted with the building of the same; and he placed them in such a curious fashion that they could not be defended without firing into one another—that is to say, the enemy, had he wished it, might have quietly encamped between the two and defied either to fire a shot. I pointed out this fact to the gallant colonel; but he assured me he had taken into consideration that the *Kaffirs* had not sufficient sense to discover this undoubted weakness in his plan.

The heights having thus become free, I next proceeded to feel the way down into the Waterkloof itself. There was no greater difficulty in this than in what I had already done; in short, the *Kaffirs* had got such a wholesome dread of my corps, that the trouble was to get near them. Before a month had elapsed in this sort of work, I had traversed the *kloof* from one end to the other; and the few sable gentlemen who still held to this home of theirs had taken refuge on the rocks on the opposite ridge, or what we used to call the Dead Man's Home, owing to the bones of some of our men remaining unburied there.

One morning, in returning from an expedition in the Waterkloof, where I had captured the few remaining cattle left to the enemy, Brigadier-General N——t, who commanded the defenceless forts constructed by Colonel ——, sent for me; and at his request I gave all the information I possessed concerning the Waterkloof, stating, among other matters, what I had done on the previous night. He said he was afraid I was doing more harm than good by this night work; it was an irregular and unmilitary mode of proceeding; that he had thought the matter over, and intended to clear the place out that day in a really effectual manner.

I warned him that the enemy was driven to desperation, and capable of mad freaks of revenge that would certainly entail serious loss if attacked during the day; and as a proof of their present state, they had that morning followed me almost into camp, and once or twice I felt convinced by their bearing they were half inclined to attack it. Now, if left to themselves for a few days longer, half starved and discouraged, they would probably leave of their own accord that part of the country. The general, however, pooh-poohed my reasoning, and shortly afterwards marched out with all his forces, composed of the 60th Rifles, the 74th, the 91st, a battery of artillery, rocket-tubes, &c.—in fact, a most formidable body of men, and equal, if properly handled, to beat easily the same number of the best troops in Europe. They proceeded towards Mundell's Peak, and I went to lie down as was my wont after passing a night out.

In the afternoon I was awakened by the sound of big guns and heavy musketry close at hand. On looking out, I saw, about a mile off, in the open, General N——t engaged with the enemy. I could easily make out that he was somewhat severely pressed, so calling for men to follow me, I made as quickly as I could to the front. I met on the way Captain S——n of the Rifles, with a party of men, axes in hand, falling back to the rear. Captain S——n cried out that I had better look to myself. He himself had been told off to cut a road into the *kloof*, but they had been driven back, and N——t was beaten. I, however, still went on; and gathering as I went some of the men who were retreating, came up to the line of fire, and faced the pursuing *Kaffirs*. When I had a sufficient number in hand to give an impetus to the movement, with a rattling cheer we went at the *Kaffirs*, who at once fell back, and eventually we pursued them almost to Mundell's Peak.

Here our real difficulties began. I had to return to the camp, but there were no supports to fall back upon; for none of the regulars, except those with me, had followed my onward movement. To increase the difficulties, there were several wounded to carry and no stretchers to lay them on. In this dilemma I sent Lieutenant H——d to ask General N——t for the required support. He did not return. I then sent Sergeant Herridge, who, after great delay, owing to the difficulty in finding the general, whom he at length discovered breakfasting, returned with the message that he had no time nor men to spare, and I must return the best way I could. Thank God, we did get back, but had a narrow squeak for it.

On the first movement I made to retire, the *Kaffirs* hurried to our left flank, near the edge of the *kloof*, to cut us off. I followed in the same direction, and that so closely that I drove the greater part of them over it; and so that effort of theirs became fruitless. While doing this others had run forward on my right flank, which was out in the open; but here also the Minie rifle did its task right well, and beat them back. Thus alternately struggling on both flanks, I got at last to some rocks about a mile from the camp. Here I halted until Lieutenant H——d, whom I now saw approaching with the men (who had, on my sudden departure, been left behind), came and relieved me of all further fears. It was now, on questioning Lieutenant H——d as to his delay— questions which were not very audible, owing to the firing still going on—that he interpreted some words amiss, and the next day, much to my regret, resigned.

After some still further delay, owing to the desperate attempts the *Kaffirs* made to turn our position, we eventually returned safely to camp, bringing all our wounded with us. After this affair I did not conceal my opinion of General N——t's conduct towards me that day; and D——e, a fine young fellow of the 74th (the "British bull-dog" they called him), thought it incumbent upon himself to ask for an explanation on the part of the regulars. This, R——y of the artillery—a thorough officer and gentleman, be it said—kindly gave him for me. He appeared satisfied, and thus the matter ended. In the report I made of this affair, I stated matters as they virtually occurred; and a few days after, an order arrived in camp from headquarters, stating that no officer of any rank whatever was to interfere with my movements, but, on the contrary, to give me whatever help I asked for; and Colonel S——t, secretary to the commander-in-chief, sent me the following, enclosed with a kind letter:—

To Captain Lakeman.

Fort Beaufort, Aug. 31, 1852.

Sir,—Having submitted your report of the 29th inst., I am directed to convey to you, by desire of the Commander of the Forces, his Excellency's satisfaction with the constant activity and military energy you have displayed since you have been engaged in the operations in the vicinity of the Waterkloof

(Signed)   A. J. Cloëte,

Quartermaster-General.

A native levy of *Fingoes* was now adjoined to my command. This strengthened my position considerably; but what gave me an absolute power over the native population of the district was an event which occurred concerning some *Kaffir* prisoners in my camp. It happened thus: While out coursing one day, a short distance from my quarters, I saw a considerable stir there going on, and ultimately a string of men went from thence to a by-path on the ridge of the hill, which led down towards Blinkwater Post. It was evidently an escort of prisoners, and I was greatly exercised by the thought of where these came from, knowing that there were none excepting those in my camp, with whom no one had the right to interfere.

I sent a man on horseback to inquire into the matter. He came back and reported that they were the very prisoners in question, and that they were being removed by General N——t's orders to Fort Beaufort. I galloped immediately back, and told the officer in command of the escort that he could not proceed: these prisoners were mine, and had been taken in an engagement in which none but my own men had been employed. They were also necessary to me for the information they could give as to the whereabouts of the rest of the tribe. After a long and painful interview of more than an hour, the prisoners were taken back to my camp, Escorted by my own men. The *Fingoes* in my new levy, after this act of mine, used to call me "Government," from, I was told, the fact of their always hearing this word spoken of in relation to Her Majesty's proclamations in the colony, which always began with, "Whereas Her Majesty's Government." But let the fact be as it may, from that day they were implicit followers of mine.

Johnny Fingo, their chief, was a tall, powerful fellow, who spoke *Kaffir* perfectly well; and passing himself off as such, used to make excursions among the tribes in revolt, and bring me back most useful information. One day, however, as if to punish me for my hardly just and certainly arrogant act in taking back the prisoners as above related, he led me into a painfully false position. He reported having found out, some seven miles on the other side of Post Reteif, the encampment of the *Kaffirs* that my night attacks had driven out of the Waterkloof. I proceeded with him and a small escort to the place indicated—a deep *kloof* in the mountains—and certainly saw a large number of fires therein.

On returning we fell in with a small outpost of the enemy, consisting of five men, who were crowded together in a rude hut, dividing among themselves some womanly apparel, evidently the fruits of plunder. Johnny Fingo, in his haste to shoot these poor devils, whom we had stealthily crept upon (having seen their campfire a long way off), forgot to put a cap on his rifle, and as the gun only snapped fire as he pulled the trigger, some three or four feet from the head of one of the disputing marauders, he received in return a lounge from an *assegai* through his thigh. The rest jumped suddenly up, and an indiscriminate *mêlée* took place.

Poor Dix received a fearful crack on the skull from a *knobkerrie* (he was never perfectly right afterwards); Johnny Fingo got another stab in the legs, and, what affected him still more, his beautiful "Westley-Richards" double-barrelled rifle, which he had obtained Heaven knows how, was irretrievably damaged. His younger brother, a smart lad, had his windpipe nearly torn out by a *Kaffir's* teeth. In short, they fought tooth and nail, like so many wild beasts. It was only after we had been all more or less scarred, that two of the five were taken prisoners, the other three not giving in till killed.

I here had an opportunity of observing the utter indifference to physical pain which the black man exhibits. Johnny, although badly wounded and unable to stand, was bemoaning his broken rifle as it lay across his knees; and while I was bandaging his brother's horribly-lacerated throat, he repeatedly asked me as to the possibility of getting the indented barrels of his rifle rebent to their original shape.

On our return to the camp I immediately set about the preparations for what I considered would be a rather hazardous undertaking—namely, to drive out the *Kaffirs* from the *kloof* in which I had lately seen them.

Anxious also to renew my relations with the regulars, after my late *mal entendu* concerning the disposal of prisoners, I proposed a joint expedition, which was eagerly accepted by Colonel H——d of the Rifle Brigade. Four days afterwards we proceeded to the spot in question, and not a *Kaffir* was to be seen, and even their traces had been carefully obliterated.

I never was more mortified in my life; it looked to me as though I had been attempting something even worse than a stupid practical joke. Colonel H——d was, however, excessively considerate in the matter, and affected to be perfectly satisfied—although but the very faintest marks of the enemy's passage could be discovered.

The country being now perfectly free for many miles around, I made long patrols to distant parts, coming at times in contact with small parties of the enemy, but too disheartened to make a stand. One night, in returning after a rather longer absence than usual, I found a somewhat large number of *Kaffirs* assembled in the abandoned village on Mundell's Peak. I may here mention that, as I always marched the men by night and reposed them by day, many rencontres of this sort occurred—that is to say, that after pursuing the foe for several days, we were often confronted in a manner as surprising to the one as to the other.

I placed the men in a straight line from one edge of the peak to the other, ordering them to lie down, and await daylight before opening fire. Stretching myself on the ground, just in front of Sergeant Shelley, I gave, at the break of day, the order to fire; when, directly afterwards, poor Shelley struggled to his feet, and fell back again, groaning fearfully. He was shot through the heels. The ball that effected this came down the line, and evidently from one of our own men—for on either flank there were sudden dips of several hundred feet, which rendered it impossible for a shot from the foe to come from thence.

This cowardly shot, which had been aimed at my own head, the men declared came from Waine. He, however, denied it so stoutly, and no one having seen him actually fire in our direction, I took no overt steps in the matter as to bringing him up for it; but I determined never to take him out again for night service. And on after-thoughts I recollected several unaccountable shots that had passed by me during our nocturnal expeditions; and although I sincerely pitied poor Shelley, I could not help feeling thankful that through the misfortune to him I had got rid of Waine. Shelley eventually recovered sufficiently to go with me to the Crimea, where he died.

The end of Waine was like a judgement upon him, as I shall now attempt to describe. Always left in camp, it was his task to clean the fire-locks when the men returned after night expeditions. This he had to do whether any firing took place or not, as the heavy dews rendered the cartridges unreliable for further use if left in the guns.

On one occasion a man gave him his firelock to clean, telling him it merely wanted wiping out, as it was unloaded. Waine did this, but could not clear the nipple, and after several attempts he took the weapon back to its owner, telling him of the fact. A cap was then put on, and Waine, holding out his hand, told him to fire, and see for himself. The man pulled the trigger, the

51

gun exploded and blew Waine's hand to pieces. It appeared that, unwittingly, it had been left loaded. Waine was removed, and shortly afterwards died of lockjaw.

CHAPTER 8

Remove to Blakeway's Farm

News now arrived in camp that the commander-in-chief, with all the forces at his disposal, consisting of several thousand British soldiers, with native levies and batteries of artillery, was expected in the neighbourhood of the Waterkloof, and to clear out that *Kaffir* stronghold which had caused the shedding of so much blood, and to some extent had tarnished, if not the fame, at least the prestige, of British arms. On the 11th July I received orders to make the necessary preparations, and on the following night to proceed to the Waterkloof, where I should be joined by Colonel Eyre with the 73rd. The 73rd were called the Cape Greyhounds. By their training they had become the most effective fighting regiment at the Cape, and had never left a wounded or dead man behind in the hands of the foe.

As might be expected, Colonel Eyre himself was a most daring, energetic officer; and Colonel H———d and he showed great promise of becoming remarkable commanders. According to the instructions I received, I started that evening to the Waterkloof; and knowing all the winding ins and outs of the place, found myself before daybreak in the centre of the *kloof*, having been opposed on my way by a few Hottentot deserters. These were readily known by the use they made of the bugle. They took refuge on the top of a solitary mound, which stood somewhat lower down in the valley, towards Mundell's Peak, and which was called the "Blacksmith's Shop," from the fact of its being the place where these same deserters (some of whom had been armourers in the Cape corps) used to repair the enemy's firelocks.

I waited where I was until ten o'clock, and seeing no appearance of Colonel Eyre, I determined to clear out the above-named shop, and there await further orders. Firstly, I was induced to do this by the Hottentots, who, seeing my inaction, had crept somewhat disagreeably close, and opened a galling fire; and secondly, by the supposition that if, by some mischance, Colonel Eyre should not appear, I was by my inaction increasing the boldness of the foe, and thereby adding to the difficulties of my retreat should I be compelled to make one. This affair took more time than I had anticipated: the day was hot, the men had eaten no food, the hill a steep one, and the Totties tenacious of their last grasp on what had been for so many months a safe home for them in the midst of a British army.

In charging up the hill, a shot came so close to my head that I confess I ducked most humbly, but was so much ashamed of this act of mine that I pretended very awkwardly to have stumbled. Scrambling hastily up, I received another shot just over the eyebrow, which whirled my helmet off, and left me bare-pated before the cheering Totties. But I, considering that more danger lay in the deadly rays of the sun than in their uncertain aim, took off my coat, and placed it round my head; and in this Red Riding-hood fashion, amidst the laughter of the men, we charged up the remainder of the hill, and drove the Totties out of the place.

Here we found some provisions, and were sitting down to the meal, when artillery opening down in the valley told us that Her Majesty's army was fighting its way up to where we were quietly breakfasting.

Colonel Eyre now appeared on the heights to our left; Brigadier B——r surveyed us at the same time on our right; Brigadier N——t looked on in our rear; while General Cathcart and his brilliant staff were espying us with their Dollonds in front, perhaps. I should have laughed outright had I not seen such things before during my Algerian campaigns, and at Astley's.

Hastily finishing our repast, gathering the prisoners together, with a few heads of cattle—not forgetting the anvil, hammer, bellows, tongs, &c., we had found in the above-mentioned shop—I proceeded to the headquarters of the commander-in-chief and reported progress. I found him toasting a chop on a ramrod. Poor General Cathcart! He was a valiant soldier, but had no more intuitive knowledge of *Kaffir* warfare than he displayed intuition against the Russians at Inkerman. His was a bold soul in a skeleton's frame; there was no material vitality in what he did; his efforts were spasmodic and unnatural. I laid down the trophies of my victory, taken from the shop, at the general's feet, and Colonel Cloëte gravely wrote down from my dictation the details of our proceedings. Prisoners and cattle were handed over to the proper authorities, and my men and I went to our quarters amidst the congratulations of all around—they, no doubt, as puzzled as myself to discover what there was worthy of thanks in our conduct that day.

As proudly, however, as so many Redan heroes, we marched off with our laurels, whatever their real value might be. But if we were so modest. General Cathcart was more outspoken; he was determined to unveil to the gaze of the world our blushing honours: a grand general order came out—Falstaff's men in buckram went down like stupid wooden-headed skittles compared to the ebony-headed niggers I had bowled over that day.

I was perfectly astounded. The general, however, had made one slight mistake in the hurry of the moment; my name had been *left out* and in its place general officers had been mentioned, getting warm thanks for the able measures they had taken for carrying out the commander-in-chief's plan to clear the Waterkloof. Those who had not that day seen a shot fired, or a prisoner taken, nor even had a distant view of the Blacksmith's Shop, were dragged before the British public as worthy recipients of well-earned thanks. This, I thought, was rather too serious a mistake, so I determined to lay the matter once more before the commander-in-chief and ask for a revision of his general order.

In furtherance of this, I proceeded to headquarters, at Graham's Town. On arrival I explained the object of my journey to Colonel S——, who told me it was perfectly right that something should be done, but he hardly knew how to set about it, and referred me to Colonel Cloëte as the proper person to apply to. I was, however, of Happy Jack's opinion, not to appeal to a subordinate when I could get a hearing from the commander; so, without more ado, I presented myself *in propriâ personâ* to the general, who was sitting in the adjoining room at the time.

After his inquiries as to the object of my journey, I asked him as quietly as the emotions then striving within me would allow, that my efforts in the late clearing out of the Waterkloof should be mentioned in the same kind manner in which he had stated my previous services—and if he thought it requisite for the public good to publish the names of officers who had not seen a shot fired that day, I hoped he would consider that my name had still juster claims for his acknowledgment. The general rose in a towering passion, exclaiming that if I did not resign immediately he would have me tried by court-martial. I replied that, if he would consent to my stating the real causes for sending in my resignation, I was ready to pen it there and then before him.

After a pause he asked me to be seated, and placing himself on a camp-stool, the old soldier began conning the matter over to himself, looking towards me at times more inquiringly than decided as to which of the two had the best of the case. His womanly weakness to please the great men at home had evidently led him to pander a little too much to their acquaintances out here, whilst I, whom he personally liked, had been unduly neglected. The thought was galling; but at last he rose, and said he had not forgotten me, but thought it better to mention my name in a different manner; and was then occupied in sending his despatches home to the Horse Guards, in which he had asked for a military appointment for me in India. "Leave me now," he added, "and tomorrow you shall have a general order also."

In fulfilment of this promise, Colonel S—— called upon me the next day, with "Here, Lakeman, is what you asked for—a general order all to yourself—while the rest of us only get mentioned in a lump. I am, however, pleased at the result of your interview with the General. I could not help hearing in the next room that it was rather hot at one time; but all's well that ends well—give us your hand." No mention by me could have done kind-hearted, brave Colonel S—— any good, dead or alive; but now that he has laid down his life for his country, he belongs somewhat to all that remain; and I wish to say how much I respected and liked him. Had he not been so much above me in station and favour, I should add still more to my panegyric.

Headquarters, Graham's Town,
October 7, 1852.

Lakeman's Volunteer Corps, from their good conduct and the gallantry of their commander, not only in the recent clearing out of the Waterkloof, but also on many previous occasions, will be called for the future the Waterkloof Rangers.

(Signed)   A. J. Cloëte,
Quartermaster-General.

Thus ended my only disagreement on military matters of this kind at the Cape. I rather cemented than otherwise my relations with the commander-in-chief, but became the acknowledged enemy of Colonel Cloëte, the quartermaster-general, who, I had good reason for believing, had been the originator of the dispute in question.

The ill-will, however, was all on his side; he had taken a great dislike, it seemed, to my method of discussing military and political matters in general; we were especially divided as to the meaning of *colonial allegiance*; and the fact of us being both of Dutch origin did not mend matters in a colony in which the in-habitants had such different objects in view as the Dutch and English settlers had.

I returned next day to the front with an offer I had in my possession from the commander-in-chief to any of the men who wished to establish themselves on the frontier as military settlers, of a small but comfortable homestead, sufficient cattle and means to begin farming with, and future help should necessity require it, on the condition of their presenting themselves for military service whenever called upon by Her Majesty's Government. I kept this offer by me, never seeing my way perfectly clear to make use of it. The men were not of the right sort to cement goodwill between natives and settlers, but the matter got winded about among them, and much increased the difficulties of my command.

On the slightest reproof they would flaunt before me their titles as farmers in prospective; and this they carried on to such a ridiculous excess, that I have known them, when under the influence of drink, attempt to turn men out of public-houses under the pretext that they were not fit associates for gentlemen farmers. I had also an order that freed me from any authority, military or civil, in the discharge of the duty of keeping clear of *Kaffirs* the district around Fort Beaufort; also another giving me the liberty of fixing my headquarters anywhere within ten miles of that place. I accordingly selected Blakeway's Farm as the most suitable spot for carrying out my instructions, and immediately removed there.

The commander-in-chief was now ready for his grand expedition into Basutoland. This carrying of the war into distant parts was, as far as I could judge, a most unwise undertaking. The colony, and more particularly its frontier, was in a far too unsettled state to receive an accession of territory with benefit to itself or profit to the land annexed; while the costly expedient of retaining several thousand British troops at the Cape for the sake of punishing Basutos, was like keeping up a large hawking establishment of peregrine falcons to chase some troublesome crows. A few police jackets stuffed with Government proclamations would have done the work equally well.

This untimely craving for excitement beyond the pale of legitimate hereditary succession has always been the bane of young colonies—and also, alas I of rapidly wearing out motherlands. A violent extension of boundaries cannot easily be justified. Violence begets violence; and nothing will rankle so much in the minds of men, from generation to generation, as the idea that they have been unjustly deprived of their forefathers' land.

CHAPTER 9

The Cruelties of War

It was during this period, while all elements of warfare at the Cape were dying of exhaustion, that I had time to observe many characteristics of the *Kaffir* race.

One remarkable trait in their character is their sterling singleness of purpose in whatever they undertake. Whatever task a *Kaffir* has in hand, he does it thoroughly—no hesitation, no swerving from the object proposed; there is a childlike belief in the possible attainment of whatever they seek, which seems incredible to those who know the folly of the searcher.

Two small pieces of stick joined together by a strip of leather, and blessed by a witchdoctor, would enable him to face death, in any shape, undismayed, secure in the thought that he possesses a talisman which renders him invulnerable.

A *Kaffir* will chase a whim, a freak, or a fancy as persistently and as eagerly as a schoolboy will chase a butterfly until he sinks from exhaustion.

I have seen a native woman seated on the ground, mirroring herself in a bit of broken glass, and vainly trying to reduce her crisp woolly locks into some faint semblance of an Englishwoman's flowing hair. Thus she would comb and comb, in the useless effort to make herself as artificial as the life she saw reflected there.

Reaction with them is naturally as intense as the previous excitement. A *Kaffir* who has been risking his life so recklessly to defend his home, will, when defeated, become wholly heedless of what remains—wife and children, goods and chattels, may perish before he will awake from his prostration and stretch out a finger to save them.

I have seen a native deserter condemned to be hanged, point to the men who were tying the noose on the branch of a tree, and explain by signs that the knot was too long for him to freely swing between the branch and the ground.

I have seen another, wounded in the leg, and unable to walk to the place of execution, when placed on my pony to carry him there, urge on the animal to the spot, and when the knot had been placed round his neck, give the *"click"* that sent the pony on and left him swinging there.

A *Kaffir* woman, driven from her hut, refuses to be burdened with her child on the march, and if placed by force in her arms, will drop the little thing on the first favourable occasion on the roadside to die.

Men and women, huddled together as prisoners after an engagement, appear utterly indifferent to one another's sufferings; the husband will not share his rations with his wife (unless ordered to do so), nor will she share hers with him.

A *Kaffir* child will ask you for the beads you have promised him for bringing you to the hut in which you are going to shoot his own father.

I have heard and seen many horrible things, but this I must say, that the most atrocious villains, and the most lovable beings on the face of God's earth, are to be found among the white men. A more kind-hearted soul than Sergeant Shelley could never be conceived; and another man in my corps used to carry about, concealed under his jacket, a broken reaping-hook, to cut the throats of the women and children we had taken prisoners on our night expeditions.

As another proof of what men may become in time of warfare, Dix one morning came to inform me that I could not have my usual bath in the small copper vat in which I had been accustomed to take my matutinal tubbing. Upon further inquiries I found that it had been used for a purpose which I will attempt to describe.

Doctor A—— of the 60th had asked my men to procure him a few native skulls of both sexes. This was a task easily accomplished. One morning they brought back to camp about two dozen heads of various ages. As these were not supposed to be in a presentable state for the doctor's acceptance, the next night they turned my vat into a caldron for the removal of superfluous flesh. And there these men sat, gravely smoking their pipes during the live-long night, and stirring round and round the heads in that seething boiler, as though they were cooking black-apple dumplings.

One morning two *Kaffir* boys, that had been found by the men marauding on the outskirts of our camp, were brought to me, and by the offer I made of blankets and beads, were led to promise they would guide us to where the rest of the tribe lay concealed in a deep glen between the stony ridges that ribbed off from the Waterkloof heights. In furtherance of this object I started with a small detachment of forty men under Lieutenant Charlton. The summit of the *kloof* was wrapped in heavy clouds, and in passing through the hoary woods which fringed the foot of the hill, grave doubts came over me as to whether I was justified (now that the war was ebbing to a close, and had taken a decided turn in our favour) in thus tempting children to betray their parents; and as these boys were cautiously feeling their way to the front, like mute slot-hounds picking up an uncertain trail, it appeared to me that we were more like revengeful pursuers hunting down poor fugitive slaves, than man going to meet man and fight out our disputed rights in fair play. God's will be done I but the task assigned to the white man is often a difficult one.

At one time he appears as a sort of legal hangman in the name of Nature's undefined laws; at another, simply a murderer; at a third time, as I hardly know which of the two. Nevertheless, one conviction always comes back with a desolating pertinacity amidst all my doubts, and that is—we never can be equals, in peace or in war; *one* of the two must give way; and as neither will do so while life lasts, Death can be the only arbitrator to settle the dispute.

Many and many a time have I held out the hand of good-fellowship to the negro, but have never felt him clasp mine with the same heartfelt return. It has either been with a diffident pressure, as though something still concealed remained between us, or with a subtle slippery clasp, which gave one the idea of a snake wriggling in the hand, seeking when and where to bite.

Thus communing with myself, I followed hesitatingly the heels of the *Kaffir* children; when they suddenly stopped, and pointing to some faint glimmering lights that appeared, in the murky atmosphere of the valley, to be far off, but in reality were close at hand, asked for the blankets I had promised, for there stood the huts in which their parents slept whom they had brought me to shoot! I halted the men, and ordered them to lie down: and there we lay, stretched out on the ground, within sixty yards of the village, watching the *Kaffirs* come out to tend their fires, and endeavour to conceal the glare, as though afraid of attracting attention, then cautiously looking round, retire to rest again inside their little branch-covered huts.

While thus lying and watching to our front, some cautious footsteps from the rear were heard approaching, and several *Kaffirs*, finding out their mistake too late to fall back, threaded their way through our ranks as though the men were but so many logs of wood instead of the deadly foes they knew us to be. The last of these stragglers was leading a horse which obliged him to stop, as the brute stood snorting over one of the men—it refused to pass by. At length it made a plunge forward, and its heels coming disagreeably close to the man's head as it landed on the other side, he rose, with a good hearty oath. The *Kaffir*, however, proceeded stolidly on his way.

These *Kaffirs* stopped at the huts and spoke to the people around them, but evidently did not communicate the knowledge of our presence to their friends, for they retired again quietly to rest. My horse, Charlie—a good, sensible animal as ever a man bestrode (it was the charger that General Cathcart had given me)—having winded the horse the *Kaffir* had lately led through our ranks, threw off the hood his head was usually covered with to prevent his attention being drawn to other cattle while we were lying in wait around villages, and began to neigh. Out swarmed the *Kaffirs* like bees aroused harshly from their hives. They evidently knew the loud neighing of my entire horse did not proceed from one of their small *Kaffir* ponies, who, in their turn, were now replying to Charlie. Before a minute had passed, our men had opened fire, and the *Kaffirs* in return were hurling back to us their *assegais*. This did not last long. With a loud cheer the huts were charged. Soon all was over; and after pulling out the dead and the wounded, we set fire to the village.

During the fight, a little *Kaffir* boy, who had been curled up in a *kaross*, had received a bullet in the sole of his foot, which, passing up the leg, had smashed several inches of the bone. As he was being rolled over and over whilst the men were dragging the *kaross* from under him, he explained to me, by signs, his impossibility to rise. He stretched out his little bronzed fingers towards me; and his childish, olive face, lit up by the glare of the fire from the burning hut, looked to me like the illuminated countenance of the infant St John which one often sees in medieval pictures, and I could not help taking up the little fellow in my arms and giving him a hearty kiss.

I could not leave him in his helpless condition; yet how were we to get him back to the camp? His leg was quite smashed. The man whom I tipped with a sovereign to carry him, found it dangling about in the most sickening manner, and at last gave up the job. The only chance left was to have an amputation performed. To this the child submitted without a murmur; and Dix, my cook, took the limb off at the knee in a manner that would have astonished a London surgeon. This was not the first "case" on which Dix had tried his "'prentice hand;" for some time past his vocation had been that of head surgeon and barber in general to the corps.

The little patient arrived eventually at the camp all right; and it may perhaps interest my readers to hear that a wooden leg was made for him, on which he used to stump off extraordinary

Kaffir reels that might have given a new idea to some of those bonnie Scotchmen who indulge in the Highland fling. But the most profitable feat for the little performer was the following:— In a small stream that flowed some two hundred yards in front of Blakeway's Farm, the men had made a large pond for bathing, by sinking the bed of the river. Over it a small platform was erected from which one might take a plunge.

To this spot the little *Kaffir* was led whenever visitors arrived at the camp (and this often occurred, now that the war was drawing to a close). There, one end of a string being tied to his wooden leg, and the other fastened to a fishing-rod, he popped into the water like a large frog, and went down to the bottom, while up rose his leg like a float. Then began the exciting struggle of landing this queer fish; and when this was achieved, amid roars of laughter, a shower of coppers was sure to make up for his ducking.

The country around Fort Beaufort had now become so free from *Kaffirs*, that the men would often, after roll-call, of an evening go in twos and threes, without their firelocks, into the town, and return again before next morning's *réveillé*, laden with *calibashes* filled with Cape-smoke. I may mention that this is the name of an intoxicating liquor made from the prickly pear or Cape cactus.

To prevent these irregular proceedings. Sergeant Herridge used to patrol the road with a party of men; and one evening he brought back an old woman, two middle-aged ones, and a young girl, whom he had found in a *kloof* adjoining the before-mentioned road. The girl was called "Noziah." We soon found out that she was no less important a personage than the sister of the *Kaffir* chief Sandilli, who, with "Macomo," was the greatest opponent to British power at the Cape. The old lady was the principal attendant, the two others the "lady-helps," of the party. The former was a most communicative personage.

After relating the splendour of the young damsel's origin, and the responsibilities under which she herself laboured, as being the *duenna* to whose care Sandilli had confided so incomparable a treasure, she asked to be allowed to go on her way, and report progress to her mighty chief. The ancient dame was quite a character, and I felt interested on her behalf; and explained, through Johnny Fingo, that she was at perfect liberty to go where she liked—adding that, during her absence, I would look after the welfare of her charge, and that Sandilli might expect to see his sister return as she had been confided to my care.

The old lady, after expressing, by profound salutations, her gratitude to me, was on the point of departing, when Sergeant Herridge remarked that she wore a wonderful necklace of lions' and leopards' teeth strung together, and that he would like to have it. On this being explained to the old woman, she stoutly refused to part with it, saying it was a charmed token, an heirloom in her family, and had belonged formerly to a great witchdoctor, of whom she was the lineal descendant. There, for the moment, ended the matter, and shortly afterwards she started on her journey alone. Sergeant Herridge was observed to follow her; and just after she had disappeared behind the brow of the hill that rose over Blakeway's Farm towards the Waterkloof, a shot was heard, and the sergeant came back with his leather jacket spattered with blood.

The next day the old woman's body was found; and as the men believed that she had been murdered by Herridge, he was in consequence shunned; for however brutally cruel many of them were, killing without mercy all that came in their way when engaged in fight, young as well as old, even braining little children—yet this was done against the supposed deadly enemies of their race, and not in cold blood for the sake of plunder.

It must not even be supposed that men could be brought into this savage state of mind without many harrowing causes of anger. I have not related the many proofs we had had of the fiendish ferocity of our foes. We had all seen the victims, or the remains, of their abominable tortures: women disembowelled, and their unborn progeny laid before them; men mutilated, and their amputated members placed in derision to adorn their yet living bodies, their wounds exposed to flies and maggots, and fated to feel death thus crawling loathsomely over them. All this had exasperated the men into frenzy. We all knew what awaited us if we fell into their power. It is true that people at home, who descant quietly on the rights of man, may have some difficulty in realising the feelings of the men.

As this supposed case of murder was not reported to me for several days, and when at last I inspected the place where the deed was said to have been committed, the old woman's body had been so much eaten up by jackals, &c., as to be no longer recognisable as to which sex it belonged, I left the matter alone. Herridge in the meantime stoutly denied to all that he had committed the crime. About a month afterwards he expressed a wish to leave the corps and rejoin the police. Knowing his, to say the least of it, uncomfortable position, I allowed him to do so, giving him letters stating the services he had rendered during the war, to facilitate his readmission into the police force, from whence he had in reality deserted.

This is one instance of the many *laches* which occurred in my corps, and which, as the authorities took no positive notice of it, I was only too glad to pretend to ignore.

On my return to England in the following spring, I was asked, on passing through Graham's Town, to go and visit a man then lying in the hospital there, and who had formerly belonged to my corps. I accordingly went, and found the man to be Sergeant Herridge. I was shocked to see the emaciated state to which his powerful frame had been reduced, and the haggard, shifting look of his once fearless eye. His right hand and arm had withered to the bone; and as he held it propped up with the other before me, he said, "That did it, sir; the Almighty has blasted it; the old woman is revenged. I knew by the look she gave me when dying that all was not settled between us; but she has never left gnawing at that arm since, and now she is sucking away at my brains. Tell me, sir, will she leave me alone when I am dead?"

Poor Herridge! His deed was a cruel one, and he suffered cruelly for it. Doctor B—— of the 12th, who attended him, remarked that he had never seen a case in which the power of the mind so visibly affected the body. When first brought under his charge, the man merely complained of rheumatism in the arm, and insisted on the fact that it was drying it up; and in the course of two months, during which he was continually staring at it, it had in effect withered to the bone.

CHAPTER 10

Angry Reception

Meanwhile Noziah had made herself very comfortable at Blakeway's Farm, and had picked up enough Dutch and English words to make her wishes known to me on most subjects. There was a certain charm about the dusky maiden, who possessed all the subtle graces of her tribe. She soon became the presiding deity of our camp. To her all appealed in time of sickness or want; none could refuse a request that came from her lips, and none was more willing than myself to submit to her winning guidance. I thought thereby I was acknowledging the influence of a power best calculated to bring all races under British sway.

As our intimacy increased, she became possessed of the fixed desire to make me the friend of her brother Sandilli. She was so persistent and persuading in this matter that I finally arranged that a party under the guidance of Johnny Fingo should proceed to that chiefs quarter, and that Noziah should be my delegate on this embassy, to arrange an interview between her brother and me.

This was not exactly in keeping with the etiquette that prevails between belligerents, and I have no doubt that legal authority could easily prove I was in the wrong. But General Cathcart was in Basutoland, and his last words before leaving had been an injunction to keep matters quiet round the Waterkloof in any way I thought most advisable.

This left me a wide margin, which I used in sending the above-named party out in an unknown direction and with a somewhat visionary object in view; for, after all, no one knew where Sandilli was, or the mood in which he might be, if found at all. So, half hesitatingly, I sent them on their way. Dix, who was a passionate admirer of the gentle sex, of all shades and shapes (always excepting his frail better-half at Cape Town), had become a devoted follower of one of Noziah's attendants, and was to have been leader of the band; his heart, however, failed him at the last moment, and he contented himself with a passionate embrace of this his latest flame, vowing, in high *Kaffir*-Dutch, that time or distance could never extinguish the fire that burnt in his breast.

Johnny Fingo was thus left in full command. He had heard that Sandilli lay somewhere concealed in the Ama Ponda Mountains, behind Fort Alice. In that direction they accordingly wended their way; and after an absence of three-and-twenty days, Noziah returned with the news that Sandilli was in the Waterkloof, not six miles off, and there awaited my coming.

Her eagerness for our interview seemed so catching, and she had such fears that her brother might decamp once more—she knew not where—that I determined to carry out her wishes immediately. I had unbounded confidence in her loyalty to me; but I had not, by any means, the same reliance on the good faith of her brother, who bore a character for fierceness and treachery by no means reassuring. However, accompanied by her, an attendant, and Dix, I started for the interview, which it was intended should take place in the rocks so often mentioned before as the Blacksmith's Shop, and which had formed so prominent a feature in General Cathcart's description of clearing out the Waterkloof.

I left Johnny Fingo in the camp. Something in his demeanour since his return, and in his manner of relating what had happened during the expedition, appeared to me suspicious. He was like a big black snake whose poisoned fangs I knew that I had extracted at one time, but I was not sure as to whether or not they had grown to be dangerous again during his late absence; at all events, I thought him safer at home than with me.

It was late at night when we arrived on the heights above the *kloof,* so I determined, after stumbling about over rocks and monkey-rope creepers for some time, to encamp where we were for the night. A most merciful dispensation of Providence it was that we did so; for not ten yards farther on we should have fallen over a perpendicular cliff several hundred feet to the bottom. In fact, we slept on the brink of a rapid slope, not ten yards in length, that led to this fearful death.

The next morning early we arrived near the rocks we were in search of; and halting in a tolerably open space, I sent on Noziah to warn her brother of our arrival. It was rather an anxious moment. I could see by the smoke still wreathing about several still-smouldering fires, that more than one party lay concealed somewhere near those huge black rocks. But whether a volley of musketry or friendly *Kaffirs* were to issue from them, I felt by the thumping of my heart that the question was being sharply debated within. However, my anxious doubting was soon over; for Noziah came back, accompanied by a tall, limping figure, who gravely held out his hand to me.

I was anxious to be on friendly terms with this man. Noziah's brother was an interesting being to me. Her courage, handsome person, and devotedness were making rapid strides into my affections; and notwithstanding that Sandilli was far from a desirable-looking acquaintance, I strove by the hearty grasp I gave him to prove how anxious I was to become better acquainted.

We now proceeded to the rocks, Dix bringing up the rear, with orders from me to shoot the first person who committed an act of open treachery. There were here about twenty *Kaffirs.* We were soon seated on the ground—Sandilli, Noziah, and myself, the centre of a circle which these men formed about us. Dix was stationed outside the circle, gun in hand. The difficulties of entering into good-fellowship with Sandilli now became apparent; for notwithstanding the beseeching looks of Noziah, he remained dumbly staring at me in the rudest manner, and I could see nothing but suppressed rage written on his ugly countenance.

71

The other members of his council—mostly old men, who remained squatted on their hands like savage grizzly bears—looked askance at me with their bloodshot eyes, as though they would like nothing better than pulling me to pieces. Feeling thus too disagreeably scrutinised, I told Dix to point his gun, as if by accident, somewhere near Sandilli's head. This movement considerably smoothed down the very distorted features of that dark gentleman. He said something in *Kaffir* to Noziah, pointing to Dix, and I told the latter to move his firelock a little on one side.

After this mute episode snuff was passed round, and the conversation opened. I explained in Dutch that I had been led to this interview with the hope of stopping further shedding of blood; that the late engagements between my men and the *Kaffirs* had been more like the slaughtering of cattle than an honest struggle between man and man; they (the *Kaffirs*) had no ammunition, and very few guns left; it was worse than madness to suppose that a piece of stick, blessed by a witchdoctor, could drive, as they pretended, the English into the sea,—in fact, I argued that it was a duty for Sandilli, and well worthy his great influence, to order his blind followers not to sacrifice themselves any longer to such a senseless enterprise.

Sandilli replied in a curious mingling of Dutch, English, and Kaffir, of which Noziah acted as interpreter, that it was not he who had begun the war: years and years ago his father had to defend his *kraal* against General Maitland on the Sunday River, many long marches from where we then sat; that from that day to this several wars had occurred between his tribe and the English; but they were always brought on in the defence of their homes. In this manner they had been successively driven from one place to another, until there was nothing left for them but the hills. They were not hillmen, but wanted the pasture-lands in the plains from whence they had been driven, and which were now given to English farmers and cowardly *Fingoes*. He, for his part, was willing to make peace, because they could not fight against my men, who attacked them by night when they slept. During the day they were not afraid, as they had proved to Sir Harry Smith. He had been told that the Basutos had been beaten by General Cathcart: it was a good thing, because they were fools not to have come to his (Sandilli's) help when he had nearly driven the English into the sea, where they came from. He added that, if Macomo was willing, they would go together and meet General Cathcart, and explain these matters to him, trusting that something like an equable arrangement might be made for those of his tribe who remained.

I promised to send on this proposal of his to General Cathcart; and it was, moreover, arranged that Noziah should remain in my camp to convey the general's reply to Sandilli when received. Noziah also made her brother swear, over some piece of stick she held before him, that she should not be sacrificed for remaining with the English (she had often told me that that disagreeable fate awaited her). To this, after many a mysterious sign and token, he agreed, to my immense relief, and the party broke up. I had felt, to say the least of it, exceedingly uneasy during the somewhat lengthy interview.

Noziah afterwards told me that one of the party had actually proposed that I should be bound and tortured to death, as a propitiation to their witchdoctors, for the spirits of those who had perished by my night attacks. It was, perhaps, the firelock of Dix, pointed towards Sandilli's head, that prevented the carrying out of this *Kaffir*-like attention.

On returning to camp I found a small party of men who had been all night seeking us. They had caught a *Kaffir*, belonging probably to Sandilli's party, seated near the spot where we had slept that night, and around which lay strewn remnants of a newspaper in which Dix had wrapped our late meal. They concluded from these shreds that we had been pitched over the cliff, and that these tokens of civilisation were all that remained of their captain, and, in revenge, they had hanged the poor devil on an adjoining tree.

It was really high time that the war should come to a speedy end. The knowledge that this end was close at hand had sadly relaxed discipline. The stirring events of war had left a craving for excitement not easily satisfied. Life had been so freely exposed, that it was looked upon as of very hazardous value. Men were ready to give or take it on the most trivial pretexts. I have seen a party of my own men firing at one another, at long distances, from behind rocks, merely to find out the range of their Minie rifles. At other times I have known them throw *assegais* at one another for the same purpose, and more than once inflict dangerous wounds.

I naturally had more difficulty in keeping my men in order than other officers experienced in that part of the colony. My men were a rougher lot, and had only enlisted for a war that they now considered finished: Lieut. H—— had resigned; Lieut. —— had been sent about his business; Lieut. P—— was often as riotous as the men; Lieut. C—— was too young and reckless to possess the tact and persistent energy necessary for the management of so unruly a set with security to himself or satisfaction to them.

CHAPTER 11

End of the War

General Cathcart now returned from his Basutoland expedition, where British soldiers proved once more their many sterling qualities. I shall not, however, attempt to describe the work done, for I had no actual share in it. The war now, so far as active operations were concerned, had virtually come to an end; my own occupation was gone. "*Grim-visaged war had smoothed his wrinkled front*," as humpbacked Richard said, and I began to seek for excitement in a quarter which had always possessed attractions for me.

Hitherto my experiences of sport at the Cape had been of a somewhat tame description, consisting of coursing and partridge-shooting, such as I had often enjoyed, though on a larger scale, in Old England. But at that time my thoughts were on larger subjects bent, and I gave myself up thoroughly to these. My battery consisted of a Lancaster double-barrelled, oval-bored rifle, of great precision and length of range, but small in calibre; a Rigby twelve-bored fowling-piece; and a double-barrelled Barnett Minie, also twelve-bored. With these I bowled over lots of fur and feather, mostly pea-fowl, stein and bush buck.

Sometimes I went in for bigger game; but as there were no lion, elephant, or buffalo within several days' journey, I was obliged to content myself with trying my 'prentice hand on some stray leopards, whose tracks I had noticed about, as well as those of wild-boar, or rather, as I believe, of farmers' pigs run wild during the war, and which in very fair numbers ploughed up the wet *kloofs* and the abandoned gardens around the farms.

There were plenty of hyenas and jackals about, but I was tired of trying to get up any excitement about them. They were a set of sneaking marauders, who used to prowl about the camp by night for the sake of the offal and scraps to be found, and who would scamper off on the slightest appearance of danger. My English spaniel, "Dash," would often *bow-wow* them almost any distance away.

Amongst other traces of game, I had observed the spoor of a leopard, or some other soft-footed member of the feline tribe, around a pool of water at the head of the *kloof* on which Blakeway's Farm was situated. It was about two miles off, in a very dank, secluded spot, almost as dark under the big cliffs and heavy foliage as an underground cavern. It was a favourite resort for blue-buck and baboons, whose footprints had stamped and puddled the ground all around. I selected a spot under a boulder of rock that advanced almost to the margin of the pool, where I placed, day after day, as I had seen it done in Algeria, branch after branch of prickly cactus, until I had made quite a porcupine shield, big enough to shelter a man. In the centre of this I dug a small circular hole, for a seat, and ensconced thereon, I one night took my place, awaiting the arrival of my supposed game.

The grandeur of the scenery, huge grey rocks, gigantic trees, and an awe-inspiring stillness which weighed upon one's spirits, made me feel extremely small in my solitary hole. The only life moving amid these gloomy surroundings was a merry singing cloud of mosquitoes, circling round and round above my head. Had I not remembered the enormous bumps their whispering kisses used to raise on my poor face, I should have felt tempted to let some of them in under the muslin I had spread across the bushes overhead, in order to have something to occupy my attention and break the monotony, were it only these denizens of the insect world.

About three hundred yards lower down in the valley I had left the attendant who usually accompanied me on my shooting expeditions. His name was Napoleon—a name given to him by the men on account of his being a native of St Helena, and from the fact of his bearing a supposed likeness to his illustrious namesake. He held in leash two half-bred Scotch deer-hounds, that were to be slipped on the report of my gun. They were fine, strong-limbed animals, capable of pulling down almost any big game. Napoleon himself was a bold, willing fellow, on whom I knew I could place entire reliance. He was as widely awake to a stray *Kaffir* as to game. I have seen him more than once, when bush-buck had been brought to bay, go in in the pluckiest manner, and, to save the dogs, often risk his own life. Bush-buck, I may mention, have fearfully pointed, spiral-shaped horns, and have been known to make fatal use of them when driven to desperation.

Thus, far from all the world, I mutely sat, communing with the great voice of Nature around, and to the faint promptings of my small nature within. I felt and remained like a log, or rather, like the sober Irishman who entreated somebody to tread on the tail of his coat, if only for the sake of getting up a mild excitement.

I was roused from this stupor by some visitors to the pool, in the shape of two little land-tortoises, that came wabbling down, one after the other, as fast as their small groggy legs would carry them. On arriving at the water's edge, they launched forth, like boats from a slip, and floated about, side by side, as lovingly as the twin ship the *Calais-Douvres* on the Channel. They were, no doubt, a newly-married couple. It might even have been their marriage trip, as they seemed as much over head and ears in love as in water. There they were, turtling about at leapfrog, heads up and tails down, in rocking-horse fashion; and now and then, as though ashamed of such mad pranks, they would dive underneath the surface, and shyly begin playing bo-peep with one another among the sedges of the pond.

But alas! all things must come to an end, and I have heard it said that even husbands and wives get tired of one another, though Hymen forbid that I should give credence to such a report! And now, at this moment, a huge bat came lazily flap-

towards the bushes, thrown on one side, that had been lately employed in the construction of the before-mentioned turret.

Once arrived there, the same habit of protecting myself, which no doubt I had acquired by imitation from French sportsmen in Algeria, led me to try and cover my rear as safely as possible. With this view I went to work most energetically, but found the task, from the nature of the obstacles I had to overcome, very disagreeable; for, as hard as I had pushed my way in, the prickly thorns seemed to combine as strongly to spur me out. This kicking against pricks once decided in my favour, by finding that I had succeeded, after all, in making room for concealment, my courage rose in the same proportion towards the foe to my front.

I not only got so excited as to make all sorts of unearthly yells to challenge the brute to stand up, to come on, &c., but actually finished by throwing bits of stick and brushwood at him, in the hopes of bringing the sulky brute to the scratch. But he was not going to be made game of, so, in despair, I left off hallooing, and called out to Dix (who, I afterwards found out, was at that moment soundly snoozing with Napoleon at the farm) to come to the rescue. These heavy-headed sleepers were not even dreaming of my state of *funk*, and, of course, did not stir.

At length, thoroughly exhausted, I laid myself flat on the ground to get a lower-level view of the horizon, and there, with my gun pointed to the front, and a stout *assegai* at my side, I awaited what might happen.

How long I remained I never knew, but it must have been a long time, for I was getting intensely cold lying on the ground covered with a heavy dew,—when, more by sound than by sight, I felt the gradual creeping of something towards me. However unmoved I might have remained until now, the loud thumping of my heart against the ground at this juncture became intolerable; so, with a loud shout, I jumped up, and, with an ominous growl, the animal bounded into the bush a few yards on my right. I at once sent a shot in that direction, which caused a fearful uproar and scattering of bushes.

Without stopping to consider, I at once sent another shot towards the same spot, and suddenly all was silent. This not being reassuring, and as I had now no positive sign to show where the brute was, I fell back, loading, towards the farm. Here I met the men coming towards me; and after hastily explaining to them the position of affairs, we proceeded, torches in hand, towards the spot, to make a fuller investigation of what had taken place.

Here we found a fine male leopard lying dead. The first bullet I fired had broken the spine, near his hind quarters; and the second shot, composed of slugs, had taken effect in the head, and proved a speedy quietus. I believe this to spoor of one afterwards.

My experience of wild-boar shooting was more profitable in the shape of hams and chine than as to actual enjoyment of what is called real sport. I could never get them to charge home; and although I have shot little porkers that have raised an awful amount of squealing, yet even the sow-mother, and the rest of the herd, would start off in the opposite direction. Once or twice it happened that they came towards me within about twenty yards, but then they would invariably be off to the right or the left. If, however, they showed so little pluck when facing the gun, they had plenty of it when opposed to dogs alone.

I have often seen them chasing mine (and they were a stout pack) for a long distance. Upon one occasion a "souzer" of pigs chased my dogs almost into the camp, and the men had to turn out to drive them off.

I never took any pleasure in shooting baboons or monkeys; and, except to defend myself on two different occasions, never fired a shot at them. On the first occasion, I had been gathering bulbs of those red-pennoned, lance-shaped flowers, which are much admired in some parts of South Africa. I had been so intent on my task that I had forgotten my dogs, that always accompanied me, now the war was virtually over, in my strolls through the country.

The dogs were a very scratched pack. They were in all about twenty, mostly of *Kaffir* origin, of various sizes, from a huge

Danish mastiff, called Woden, to my little Sussex spaniel Dash. The ruling spirits were four Scotch deer-hounds, three of which I had purchased from Mr Andersen, my Norwegian friend at Cape Town. The other had been given to me by P——r of the Commissariat. Dhula, the biggest and bravest of Andersen's Scotch leash, would not only pull down the largest bush-buck, but would also keep guard afterwards, and prevent my *Kaffir* dogs eating it. Many an antelope had he thus saved to grace our frugal board, and to afford a display of Dix's culinary art. Poor Dhula! his life was embittered by his jealousy of Woden. The latter, although a heavy dog, ran well; and often, while chasing, when the chance offered, he would run at Dhula, and, striking him under the shoulder as he would a deer, bowl the astonished Scotch giant over and over, much to the latter's disgust.

Woden evidently could never quite understand the humour of his Scotch congener. He generally gave in to Dhula, but often after several sharp bouts, in which he always carried off the worst of the biting in the heavy folds of his shaggy throat. My *Kaffir* greyhounds would run anything and eat anything they caught, from a startled quail to a porcupine. They were as crafty as they were cruel and fleet, and in the woods ran as much by scent as by sight. They were not, however, equal in speed to my English dogs.

My plucky little friend Dash was (considering his small offensive powers) the bravest of the brave; for his winning way of bringing stones or anything else he could pick up to you, whenever he wanted a caress, or some little tit-bit to eat, had completely ground down his teeth to an unbrushable size. If it came to a regular go-in with some struggling beast brought to bay, Dash would lie down, and, twisting his knowing head about as the various ups and downs of the fight took place, looked like an old amateur boxer observing professional gluttons at work. Dash was buried on Blakeway's *kloof*, which had so often echoed to his lively tongue. A blue-faced baboon, as I am now going to relate, was the malevolent spirit which loosened all his worldly ties between his much-attached master and his love for all sports—for Dash was as much alive to the pleasure of hunting rats at a farm-rick in Old England as in chasing jackals and hyenas round our camp at the Cape.

To resume my narrative, however. As above stated, in the ardour of digging bulbs, I had forgotten my dogs, when Napoleon called my attention to their baying far down in the recesses of the *kloof*. Hastily picking up my gun, lying close at hand, and he hurriedly cramming without mercy into a sack my green-grocery-looking bunches of roots, we started off in hot haste to the spot to which the dogs were calling our attention. On our way we met them coming back; they were, however, eagerly enough disposed to return, so that we knew by that sign the object of their late *rencontre* was not supposed by them to be very far off.

And so it was, for we soon found ourselves amidst a grinning lot of large, brown, Cape baboons. They were clinging up aloft to the graceful creepers that festoon so beautifully the trees in South African woods, and looking like so many hideous, hairy-bellied spiders on a beautiful lace-work of Nature's weaving. I felt inclined to give some of them, who looked particularly out of place in that sylvan retreat, a peppering of shot; but their wonderful performances on the tight-ropes around them soon smoothed the wrinkles of my indignation. These acrobats performed extraordinary feats. They shot from branch to branch, from wave to wave, like flying-fish, or as pantless Zazel shoots from the cannon's mouth to her swinging rope.

This performance created intense excitement, and the barking of the dogs seemed to applaud this aerial description of St Vitus's Dance. It was really affecting to see the solicitude of the parents as their little progeny hopped from tree to tree after them, now holding out their arms to receive them as they landed, now thrusting back a creeper to bring it nearer within their reach. It was a real exhibition of baboon agility, of which we see but a faint parody in the Westminster Aquarium, by the Darwinian selections among the human bipeds.

An accident befalling a clumsy little fellow as he stumbled on the branch of an iron-wood tree, he came to the ground with a thud. In one minute the poor chap was torn to pieces by the dogs. This was more than his parents could stand; down they came to the ground, followed closely by the rest of the tribe, and a real battle ensued between them and the dogs.

The baboons got the best of the fight,—poor Woden was ridden off the field by two jabbering jockeys on his back, who laboured his sides most unmercifully with tooth and nail. Dhula was too nimble and clever with his teeth to be caught, nevertheless he had to submit from his many persecutors with the loss of several inches of his tail. Fly, a remarkably fine red *Kaffir* bitch, which I afterwards took home and gave to the zoological gardens, was ripped up and her sides laid bare. But the worst of all occurred to poor Dash: he was carried off by a huge baboon almost as big as a totty, and I arrived to his rescue too late. I saw that he was dead, and forthwith shot his destroyer upon him. Napoleon made good use of his *assegai* and my spade; and after a fight far more exciting than glorious, we remained masters of the field.

I am thoroughly convinced, had the baboons shown any unity of action, I should not have been relating this incident today.

These are about the only events in my sporting life at the Cape worthy of narration; many milder incidents occurred which I pass over, judging them insufficient to be of interest to the reader.

I know but little about snakes—they were of almost every day acquaintance; but as neither my men nor I were ever bitten by one, I have nothing sensational to write about them. One short episode I may perhaps relate. In creeping over some rocks to have a shot at a stein-buck, I cautiously looked over a ledge of stone, and fancying there was a curious garlic smell about the place, I looked down, and there, lazily stretched out at full length, almost touching my throat, was a huge *cobra di capello*. I drew back much less hesitatingly than I had peeped, and, retiring a few feet, shot it as it was rearing its head in the act of preparing to strike.

This little event gave the hitherto slight attention I had paid them a more repulsive form, and ever afterwards I destroyed all that came in my way. Up to that day I had handled them as I had seen others do—henceforth their touch became too loathsome. *Kaffirs* believe that after a puff-adder, whip-snake, or cobra has bitten, it must within a short space of time wash out its mouth with water (which these snakes invariably do, if it is at hand), else it would die from the poison that oozes afterwards from its fangs. They also think that white men, if bitten by snakes, invariably cause the death of the snake itself—for they say the white man's blood is poisonous to all serpents.

CHAPTER 12

I Embark for Cape Town

Kaffir witchcraft assumes so many fantastic forms, that it is difficult to give a notion as to any guiding principle in it. Hatred of the European seems to play a large part in all their superstitions.

A piece of stick is supposed, after blessing and incantations, to become a talisman, having the power to save the wearer from all danger the white man can attempt to inflict against him; but it is thought to be powerless in warding off a danger coming from a neighbouring tribe. They believe that we are born of the foam of the sea, and we should all perish if driven back to our ships, which they suppose to be the cradles in which we are brought up. Like almost all magicians, they believe they can raise plagues of all sorts, and inflict sores and different forms of leprosy by merely casting an evil eye upon any one.

Their knowledge of medicine and surgery is greater than may be supposed. I have known them cure headaches and neuralgia, hitherto incurable, by putting a leather band round the head, and adding underneath small smooth pebbles at certain distances, then placing a weight upon the head, which is usually a bowl of supposed mesmerised water, weighing down the whole until the head becomes completely numbed, and all pain ceases.

Two or three applications of this nature I know to be, from actual observation, a positive cure. They also know the use of several medicines, such as emetics, &c.; and in surgery will stop the bleeding of an artery as well as any surgeon—applying wet bandages wrapped round smooth stones, which act as efficiently as a tourniquet. They will also amputate the small joints with great skill.

The *Kaffir* customs are far more artificial than one would suppose from his ease of manner; every position of the body has been taught him from his childhood. Whenever *Kaffir* men or women present themselves before you, it is in the attitude they have been instructed as the most becoming for the furtherance of their wishes. A man who comes to ask for a favour which concerns the welfare of any member of his family, takes quite a different attitude than when offering to exchange something in barter. The young man who seeks to purchase the hand of his wife, has certain modes of well-defined expression in the attitude he assumes, whether hesitating or assured of success.

The triumphal swagger of a suitor who has been successful in such a mission is something marvellous to behold—it really seems as if he thought the earth would soil his feet as he treads upon it. On the other hand, if he has been refused, and has no hopes of making a second more enticing offer, he will retire in such hang-dog fashion as to make his worst enemy inclined to pity him. The man who stands before you leaning gracefully upon his *assegai*, in a posture that even a sculptor might dream of as the embodiment of manhood and grace, is not what you might suppose in a position taught by nature's school, but the summing up of what generations have thought to be the *beau-ideal* of a man.

Johnny Fingo once presented himself before me in so calm and dignified a manner that he quite surprised me; and upon my asking him the nature of the business he came upon, he replied that he was the bearer of a communication from Sandilli. No Roman presenting himself on the part of the senate, bringing an offer of peace or war to a foreign potentate, could have done so with more calm assurance of the mighty import of his mission.

The women are small in shape and frame compared with the men, and extremely beautiful, as far as the moulding of the

Two days afterwards I embarked in the *Mary Jane*, and found her to be a smack of forty tons. A long time ago she had been a trawler, but was now employed in the more important service of a Government transport.

Captain Rowe I have already partly described. I will only add that he was dark-haired, fair-skinned, grey-eyed, about 5 feet 8 inches in height, broad-shouldered, with well-rounded limbs, daring to folly (but his folly had a method in it); and his sheet-anchor a Bible, and a stout-hearted Devonshire matron at home.

He had been in his youth first mate of an Indiaman, afterwards captain of a fruiterer, and now he was the commander of what had once been his father's craft, then called the *Seagull*, but now rebaptised the *Mary Jane*. At home he had not found trawling a very profitable business, so with three other west-countrymen he had started with his little craft to barter with the natives on the West African coast.

How he got there was rather surprising. His only chronometer was his father's old watch. He took no observations, but merely guessed at his position from the distance run and the log. Occasionally he took soundings—*i. e.*, when he could find them; chart he had none. Small success had, however, attended his bold efforts, although he had several very grand "specs" on hand. In the hold were a lot of real Birmingham guns, bought at 7s. 6d. apiece, which had but one fault, that of sometimes sending off their contents at the wrong end, hitting the shooter instead of the object shot at.

There were also scores of magnificent crowns for African kings, made up of tinsel paper, brass spikes, wax pearls, and glass diamonds. He had even once, he said, furnished a mighty Ashantee potentate with a throne. This, however, he seemed to regret, it having been an old family piece of furniture. Strange as this may seem, I believed it to be quite true, as the throne in question was merely an old armchair, the legs, arms, and back of which had been severely shaken and cracked by many a toss and tumble in the cabin of the *Mary Jane*.

On my expressing surprise at his placing so shaky a seat for the support of a king, he with a sharp twinkle of the eye replied, "That is the lookout of the occupant; and," added he, "these old-fashioned articles, if spliced at the proper time and place, still last for some good length of time." Sam, like myself, was a stanch conservative, and preferred to patch his coat all over to turning it. Not that he preferred an old coat to a new one, but he liked the old constitutional cut.

Notwithstanding all his grand undertakings. Captain Sam had not succeeded as he wished, and he thought that he had been humbugging and humbugged enough. After struggling for two long years through fevers on land and heavy surf-breakers on the shore, he had finally reached Cape Town, from whence he was now engaged in carrying Government stores along the coast as far as Natal.

These and many similar yarns were spun in the cabin of Sam's little craft, in which I was now cooped up, in an atmosphere which I found fearfully clammy and stuffy after inhaling *le grand air* for two years on African uplands. Sam, however, did all he could to cheer the comfortless surroundings of his small cribbed cabin by the ever-varying novelty of his yarns. He related many a hard-fought fight with the storms of old ocean, to which, in spite of all, he still clung, and with which he still hoped to have many a tussle ere he was piped to settle his own long account.

When wearying sometimes with his tales, and the sound of the surges striking the thin wooden sides of the trembling *Mary Jane*, I would go upon deck, and there watch the long rolling waves that sweep round the Cape, or listen to the cheery voice of his sailor-boy, as he sang many a ditty of Cornish and Devon heroes, and the glorious deeds of Drake on the Spanish main.

In this way we furrowed our way along, making very wet weather round the coasts until we came to the spot where the Birkenhead had gone down so recently with all hands. Here we luffed up for a time, and, baring our brows to the breeze, offered a parting salute to the gallant crew and stout-hearted red-jackets who had here gone to their last account at duty's call; then, sheering off once more, filled our sails to a half gale of wind, and bounded off like a startled seagull towards Table Bay.

After this fashion we sped on through the sea, throwing up ridges high above our decks, and on the 12th July rounded the Lion's Mountain. Here becalmed for a time we stayed our course, when a heavy puff from the crest of that huge emblem of African life sent such a staggering pressure on our outspread canvas as nearly brought us to grief. With a sudden whirl we were on our beam-ends! My berth on board had never been very dry, but now I rolled into one still more watery in the lee-scuppers. By good luck the tackling gave way, the topsails went overboard, and the stout craft righted again, as Captain Sam expressed it, none the worse for a little deck-swabbing. I managed also to regain my place on board, none the worse for my startling bath.

The next morning I declined to land in Captain Sam's little punt, much to his annoyance, as he volunteered himself to pull me ashore. I, however, gave him to understand that it was beneath the dignity of two such west-country commanders as we were to land in such a tub-looking receptacle. The fact is, after Sam had placed his own burly person in the centre of his boat, I saw no place except his own brawny shoulders on which I could perch.

CHAPTER 13

The Voyage Home

On landing at Cape Town, I soon found that quite a different feeling existed regarding my dealings with the *Kaffirs* from the views taken of them in the eastern portion of the colony.

Here there were no burnt homesteads, despoiled farms, or murdered occupants to bring the horrors of war in a vivid manner before people. Merchants, who were enriching themselves by the money poured into the colony from Old England, considered, no doubt, the stagnation likely to ensue from the cessation of this golden stream.

Then, again, a pious class of Christians who had been devoutly praying for the Lord's mercy upon all men, both for those who were cutting, and those who were having their throats cut, could hardly conceive how I had had the courage to hang, as report said, Hottentot deserters.

Had they been Englishmen, taken red-handed in the deed, as the Hottentots were, it might have been right; but that I should have hung these missionary converts, whose only conception of brotherhood was to perform the part of Cain, seemed beyond their understanding of what was due to benighted niggers.

It is strange to remark the emulation that exists among Christian sects in their attempts to convert heathens to Christianity. The object is pursued with much zeal, but with no adequate knowledge of the work, or how it ought to be carried on. I feel convinced that it is promoted, like a good deal of home charity, not from any purer motives than may be found in self or sect ostentation. Some people who would sell their own souls over the counter if anyone would buy them, will often give their gold freely for baying over to Christianity that of a nigger.

The clergy and other high dignitaries of the Church, instead of attending to their starving flocks at home, look "*to fresh fields and pastures new*," to try and tempt straggling black sheep to the fold. So lately as a month ago—I write in November 1879—a learned chief of the Protestant faith was engaged on a long voyage of several hundred miles to confirm a sinner.

As I was a party to the pious ceremony in question, perhaps I may be allowed to relate how it took place. This stray sheep, brought back to the fold on the back of a shepherd that had once belonged to the unbelieving community, had but the merest notion of the language of the religion to which he had been so happily converted. As this innocent lamb knelt before the attentive observers, he looked like an old bearded goat of quite a different flock. The proceedings were carried on in a most mysterious manner: the bishop put the questions through the convert's spiritual prompter, the Rev. Mr H——, who in his turn gave the cue to the principal actor.

But this complicated by-play brought on a crisis; the prompter himself got confused, and hallooed out loud enough for the spectators to hear, "But who *was* your godfather?" to which query the repentant sinner murmured "De Devil!" This was almost too much for the bishop himself, and several times he was evidently in doubts as to whether or not he ought to give his spiritual blessing to such a child of the flesh. However, the ceremony was finally gone through, to everybody's satisfaction and relief.

In former years, conversions were carried on far more rapidly, and on a much larger scale. The British consulates in the East used to give a certificate of baptism and a certificate of British nationality at the same time, for a moderate sum. I remember when, in the year 1854, I was commandant of the town of Bucharest, a deputation of Jewish converts to Christianity waited upon me for help. They complained that their pastor, the Rev.

Mr M——s, had abandoned his sheep at home, and gone to sell sheepskin jackets to the British army in the Crimea. These poor forlorn wanderers added, that if I could not help them with pecuniary assistance, they would strike and knock off" work as Christians, returning to their old faith. On considering the price asked, and the value of what was proffered, I advised them strongly to do as they said, not feeling justified in spending a shilling upon them.

The East is a difficult labyrinth for a man to find his way through, there are so many finger-posts having political meanings, so many cross-paths of various denominations leading to heaven knows where!—lovely by-lanes, with all the delights of the world on their flowery banks, that men, bewildered and in despair, put up too often at the half-way houses on the road, making themselves as happy as they can with all the worldly joys around them; it is often the devil to pay—but, alas I many thousand freethinkers do not hesitate to do it. The only result of such a competition for converts is to separate men more widely than ever.

This is not my opinion alone. I had, in the presence of the English bishop above mentioned, a conversation with the Metropolitan of the Greek Church of the East. I was alluding, in the name of the Protestant divine, to the regret experienced as to the divisions existing in the church of our Lord. The exact words of the Metropolitan, and which I am authorised to state, were as follows:—

Tell his eminence of the Anglican Church that it is not the flock of Christ which is so wayward; it is we shepherds who drive them about in different directions for our own profit. What would become of me, Metropolitan of a Greek church, if his eminence could convert them to Protestantism? What would become of him if I could convert his sheep to orthodoxy? And it is so with all churches: they, the congregations, could be brought easily to assemble and be thankful to God in one mode of faith, but it cannot take place because we shepherds have an interest in dividing them.

This fearless expounder of the truth afterwards added, in reply to the bishop's desire that a prayer should be offered up by the clergy for the union of the Christian Churches in one: "God would not listen to our prayers: our kingdom, the kingdom of the priests, has been in all times a worldly kingdom; that to come will, I believe, belong to the poor. If these latter were to ask, God would listen to them, but not to us who cannot sincerely pray for such an end that would be the destruction of priestly power.

I will, (he added) give you an instance of the intricacies of the question. I who hold in my own hand some of the threads, cannot surmise a real clue to the solution, but would, as a curiosity, like to explain what I know of them. On a late visit to Paris I went in full canonical dress, and assisted at High Mass in Notre Dame. The ceremony was a grand one; the Cardinal Archbishop of Paris himself officiated. I knew but little of the rites and ceremonies he went through, but when he bowed or knelt I did the same. When he prayed, I joined in the prayer; when he blessed, I bowed my head and asked inwardly his blessing. I felt the devotion of all around, and I joined my gratitude to the Giver of all mercies.

The ceremony over, I went to the usual room behind the altar for disrobing, and was disrobed by canonical officials, as though I had been one of the chiefs in the church. I believe, from what I have heard since, that no one was offended by the manner in which I assumed a somewhat prominent part.

The next day I went in my official robes as a Metropolitan of the Eastern Church, and attended by the acolytes usual on official occasions, to pay a visit to the Cardinal Archbishop himself. *He would not receive me.* No doubt orders had been sent from elsewhere forbidding an official recognition of my position in a church at all events equal in antiquity to his own.

You see what divisions sever the leaders; how then can we expect the flock to follow them into one fold? No, no; we priests divide in order to reign. Unity of the church can only be obtained by people going to Christ without waiting for us. None of us can define, with convincing simplicity to the masses, what authority we really possess as delegates of our Saviour. I for my part am willing to hold out the hand of fellowship to all men, even to those erring brethren the Jews. In a few days I shall pronounce in the Senate a speech in favour of their admission into this country as citizens.

I must confess that in this I have listened more to the voice of Christianity in the West than in this part of the world. It is difficult for us Roumanians to look upon the Jew as a brother who looks upon our Saviour as an impostor. Yet still I have persuaded myself to perform this ill-defined task. I only trust in God that the passing of the measure will not tend to increase free-thinking doubt. I would even open my seminaries to the Jews, so much do I long to see all men brethren, but they would not come to them; neither do I regret it, for the orthodox church ought, I think, to remain in the present what she has been in the past—a prudent, wise, and charitable mother, seeking to govern her own children wisely, leaving other churches to do the same with theirs.

I shall go to England next year if my health allow; and although I shall try and convert no one, I hope there will be no necessity for conversion to convince English prelates that they have in me a true Christian brother.

The English prelate was a kind-hearted, learned man, full to overflowing with a wish to do good, but evidently puzzled how to set about it. There is a patriarchal vigour about some of the older forms of belief, which, in its racy *bonhomie*, dwarfs Anglicanism considerably, and makes it look somewhat of a sect— true, a good one, as, from the power and influence at its disposal,

Both Dutch and English present as fine specimens of our common Protestantism, and are as enthusiastic lovers of constitutional rights, as are to be found anywhere. The fault hitherto impeding their useful amalgamation has been the forcing process employed by the Home Government.

The annexation of the Transvaal has been a most immature and ill-devised proceeding. However good the wished-for object may be in itself, the end can never justify violence; and the ten thousand Dutch Boers, born and bred with the same prevalent ideas as existed during the Puritan times at home, cannot, by a stroke of the pen, be brought into allegiance to the British Crown. The native population are slowly disappearing, like dark clouds at sunrise. The advent of the white man dispels all visions of the land ever returning to the blindness and horrors of a barbarian sway. Let those who dream of admixture of races look to the difficulties at home, and hold their peace.

CHAPTER 15

Salute the Native Soil

We had a fine passage as far as St Helena. The *Arethusa* was a fast sailer and a good sea boat, although rather crank at times under the press of canvas we sometimes induced our good-natured Captain B—— to clap on her lofty spars; in fact she was overmasted, and required all that nice attention as to trimming that a top-heavy *belle* of the seas must have not to show too much of her keel.

From St Helena we sailed towards Ascension, noted for its turtle. The island itself is a dull, brown spot lying in the sea, its cracked surface looking like a burnt egg-shell. This place was discovered by Jan de Noves, a Portuguese navigator, on Ascension Day, 1501—hence its name—at least so I was told by a whitey-brown native who boarded us.

We had now arrived somewhat near the "horse" latitudes, and in calm weather, and with no work to kill the time, we began some horse-play with the monkeys on board. The name given to these latitudes arose from the number of horses the Spaniards used to throw overboard when becalmed—sometimes for weeks—in these regions, passing to and fro between their South American possessions and Europe. The chief object of our fan on board was a large, greenish, long-tailed monkey, who, with Darwinian fore-thought, had pitched upon young C—— as the fittest selection Providence had placed within his reach on the high seas. The competition as to natural fitness was so close between the two, that it was often a cause of serious dispute as to which should have his way.

One day, after a sharp bout of this kind, a real quarrel ensued, as will occur sometimes in the best-regulated families; and young C——, who prided himself much on ancestral descent, as, no doubt, did also his still more anciently descended rival, came to a regular stand-up fight with the monkey. Strength was on the side of C——, whilst cunning and skill were on the side of the old un; but at last the upstart gave his ancient *confrère* such a tremendous upper cut, as he was holding on to the rat-lines, near the bulwark, that he was knocked out of time into the bosom of the impenetrable deep, and poor young Ben (that was the name of our monkey) had to swim for it.

As this typical representative of lost nationality and universal brotherhood breasted the waves like a corker, we tried to lower a boat; but although the apparatus always acts at home, it never does at sea, so the boat stuck up in the air on its davits. We then threw a life-belt towards the now nearly exhausted Ben; but although he had enough instinct to grasp it, he had not enough sense to pass it over his head and under his arms. So we saw his efforts getting slowly weaker and weaker as he clasped and clutched at the slippery buoy, and at length he sank beneath the waves, down, down among the dead men, to be found again, no doubt, one day by some yet undreamt-of ethno-geologist, who will perhaps deduce from his bones that the aborigines of the Atlantic were very little men, with long caudal appendages, and descant learnedly upon every link in that long tail, until he comes to the end of his own, and finds out his mistake.

In commemoration of this sad event we proposed a sort of Irish wake, to be held as we passed the line.

From Ascension we reached away so far to the west that nothing but the most abstract calculation could give our captain any idea as to the latitude and longitude in which we really were, and our little bark seemed to be dancing about on the line like an amateur rope-dancer. This is a rather metaphysical metaphor; but I am talking learnedly now, influenced, no doubt, by our skipper's tuition. Time hanging heavily on my hands in this dead calm, when even the green waves assumed the lifeless heaviness of molten lead, I had taught myself navigation, and held such lengthy discussions with our captain as to the position and value of stars, planets, and constellations, as to appear to the somewhat astonished listeners around as though I were a Newton and a Pascal rolled into one.

The captain and I, over our glasses (telescopes I mean, of course), had become so awfully knowing, that my only doubts were as to which knew the least of the two; and it was only for the sake of the respect due to seniority in this happy ignorance that I allowed him to navigate the ship. One day, however, nettled by some critical observations of mine, in a sudden fit of displeasure he threw up his commission as skipper, and I took his place; but as it happened to be a dead calm at the time, I had no means of showing my superior seamanship. Thus time passed on, while I still retained a certain happy-go-lucky faith in my own *star* quite as strong as the captain's in his. In this I was fully justified, as the sequel will show.

On passing over the supposed line, which our captain, after dinner, had kindly chalked out before us in a very zigzag manner on the mahogany, in the prelude to the *in memoriam* wake for poor Ben, whom, as I previously stated, we had left deep down in the phosphorescent waters of the southern hemisphere. While others were singing song after song in happy oblivion of past warfare at the Cape, *I* was thinking that we had entered into British waters. This was somewhat a stretch of imagination, but nothing is too big for me when I dream of Old England—like Ben, I dive into futurity. Thus human nature seeks for pleasure and enjoyment in many and varied channels, according to its own appreciation of wherein these consist.

The bottle was circling freely, and the hot, stifling atmosphere of the mess-cabin below made us feel delightfully dry every time it neared us, as one after another we passed the Rubicon between self-possession and being possessed. Notwithstanding all this joviality, an uncomfortable feeling was slowly creeping over me, and at last became so unbearable that I ran upon deck to breathe the fresh air. How grand all appeared under that mighty dome, compared to the rafters of the cabin below! The night was glorious in its starry splendour; the sea slept gently heaving, as though with loving dreams surging, while soft breezes rippled its face with smiles.

The boisterous mirth arising from the cabin below seemed strangely out of place. I turned to the man at the helm; the idiot seemed as screwed as the wheel that rolled in his slackened grasp. "Holloa, mate" I said, "what is that light on the water you are steering for?" pointing to a flame I saw gleaming there.

"A tar-barrel," he said, "some chaps passing the line have chucked overboard."

"But it is nearing us too fast for that—look out, man! Good God! it's a ship!—luff, luff!" and suiting the action to the word, I jumped to the wheel and jammed the helm down; then swiftly glided by a huge black hull, its deck crowded with dusky figures, shouting and gesticulating to us like demons, its stern grazing our quarter, as the good ship *Arethusa*, like a form endowed with life, sprang up into the wind, and saved herself from destruction. One second more and we had been down, down amongst the dead men, not far from poor Ben.

Up rushed the startled convivialists from below, some with their glasses still in hand, and I crept 'neath the bulwarks, and kneeling, felt a mother's prayer had been heard that night on my behalf. This vessel proved to be the *Mauritius*, a large iron screw, then bound on her first voyage to India round the Cape. She was afterwards one of the fleet of transports placed under my orders for the conveyance of troops to the Crimea, an account of which will shortly appear in my military correspondence concerning that war. This narrow squeak sobered us for a few days, but our spirits revived as the western winds now began to blow.

The frigate-hawk—a truly wonderful bird for its powers of flight—came often to pay us a visit, and changed the monotony of continually looking into the sea for beings endowed with life. I might have shot one or two, and had the head of my rifle more than once on their bodies, as they floated overhead without a quiver in their outspread wings; but such aerial life I did not like to see streaked with blood, so I left them alone in their boundless home, instead of sending them to a glass cage in the British Museum.

Of shark, *bonito*, and other scaly-looking denizens of the sea, there had been often exciting scenes of what some called sport, but I must say I never could see much fun in it. I certainly should have liked to have had a go-in with a vicious-looking shark on fair terms, but then I was most undeniably afraid of him in the water, and on the deck of our ship he was no match for me; so, before I had seen two such hooked monsters hauled on board and butchered with spears and knives, I used to feel rather disgusted than otherwise with such displays.

As for the huge, gaunt-looking albatross as they flapped their leather-looking wings like vampires around us, no one seemed particularly anxious to settle accounts with them: a superstitious awe influenced even the most reckless amongst us as they circled above our heads. Curiously enough, the only one who had the courage to pull a trigger at them was young K—— of the 74th, and he died soon after he landed.

We were now in latitudes where westerly gales are of frequent occurrence, and a rattling one caught us one night as we were running with studding-sails set. So sudden was its approach that there could be no question of our taking in sail; so, in a storm of wind and rain, we flew along as though Neptune on his foaming sea-horses was trying to catch us. The poor little *Arethusa* fairly staggered under the force of the gale, like a startled hare now swerving to the right, now to the left, twisting, cracking, and burying herself in the sea as deep as she could without absolutely giving up the struggle and going once for all to the bottom, until old blustering Boreas at last, in kind compassion, relieved us of some spars.

Then, with the rags of our late flaunting sails, and with just as much more as was necessary to steady us on our course, we proceeded more safely if more humbly than before. The little ship rose buoyant to the seas as though no longer afraid of them, starting afresh from the top and sliding down the ribbed backs of the long-rolling billows, defying them as they crested their foaming heads in anger behind us.

It was very exciting. I thought of Sam Rowe and his little smack battling with such weather, and though I had more confidence in his skill than in that of our skipper, yet, like Tom Bowling, I preferred the *Arethusa* in the Bay of Biscay to the *Mary Jane*.

Good old Sam! I hope he won't think me foolish as he reads these lines—for the old boy is hale and hearty yet, and, with spectacles on nose, and *Western Times* in hand, can still discuss matters shrewdly.

On the 30th July the white cliffs of Brighton gladdened our eyes, and running up the coast, we hove to off Eastbourne and took a pilot on board. Some of us were so anxious to get ashore that we took passage in the boat that had brought out the pilot, and with a cheer from some of the more patient who had remained on deck, pulled away to the beach; but on our arrival there, we found that the boat was too deep in the water to get close in to the shore. This did not stop us. Young L—— and I jumped into the surf up to our waists and waded ashore. This ducking had in no wise cooled my excitement, for, in placing my foot once more on English soil, I threw myself on the ground and gave it a hearty kiss.

After this exhibition I felt rather taken aback by the astonished looks of some sightseers who had come down to view our disembarkation. On rising to explain matters to the astonished natives I could not get a word out. They no doubt thought me to be choking with emotion, but it was otherwise. In the fervour of my embrace the sand had got into my mouth, and, as I had no toothbrush at hand, I was obliged to make use of my finger to remove a lump of my fatherland from my mouth, as though it had been a quid.

Young L——, who jumped with me from the boat, had also gone through the same kissing ceremony; he, however, had not taken such a greedy mouthful, and after carefully wiping the salt water from his boots and trousers with his handkerchief, kindly offered to perform the same operation for me. To this I consented; but I thought he was paying rather too much solicitude to my appearance as he scrubbed away at my face; however, the task once over, we started for the parade, to the laughing astonishment of all the bystanders. After proceeding a little distance L—— left me on some frivolous pretext, and I went on alone.

On reaching the parade, among the first persons I met were Lady P—— and her daughters—intimate friends of my family. Without much hesitation I gave the old lady a kiss, and would have continued the salute all round if allowed, had not the expression, or rather impression, on her ladyship's face made me hesitate. She had a marbled forehead, a black-spotted nose, and a comically shaped O round her lips. I saw that I must have blackened her face; and as I knew that it could not have been done by any African black imported from the *Kaffirs*, I recollected that it must have been by some of Day & Martin's received from L——'s pocket-handkerchief as we made our hurried toilet on the beach. Lady P—— kindly accepted my excuses for this uncalled-for display of polished attention, and after a few words of explanation, left me spotless of any design to darken either her face or her fame.

On arriving in London I continued busy for some days in forwarding my importations, bulbs, and plants to my home, at that time at Grange-wood, Leicester; and the springbok, monkeys, &c., to the "Zoo" in Regent's Park.

My first serious business after my arrival was to bring the disgraceful condition of the great Napoleon's last residence to the attention of Her Majesty's Government. Every time my thoughts travelled back to my late undertakings in South Africa they passed over St Helena, and recoiled with shame at the desolate state into which England had allowed this place to fall. I, however, had not a voice loud enough to be heard at the time, and notwithstanding my repeated efforts in that direction, I could not get a member of the government during the Gladstonian era to take the matter up.

ping its wings, like a seagull, over the water, and warned, I presume, the innocent creatures that night was approaching, and that it was time for respectable couples to seek the security of their own homes. So they left their luxurious water-couch, and wabbled off, as demurely as Darby and Joan going to evening chapel.

Meanwhile evening was putting up its revolving shutters, leaving me more and more benighted, and my thoughts were turned into another direction by catching at intervals the distant barking of the bush-buck, as they replied to one another, and who, like most swaggering challengers, kept each other at a respectful distance. A distant hum arose from the direction of the camp, as confused as the medley of races it contained—Russian, Swede, French, German, English, and Dutch—men from all climes, held strangely together by the mere force of my frail will.

This thought, and other equally dim ones, occupied my mind, when the loud lapping of water close at hand caught my attentive ear, and brought me, with a startling throb, to the realities of my then actual under-taking. Straining my eyes in the direction from whence the sound came, I fancied, in the dusk, I could trace the outline of a beast of some sort on the brink of the pond. Slowly raising my gun in that direction, I was on the point of pulling the trigger, when the sound of lapping ceased.

Grave doubts now arose in my mind as to whether that at which I was levelling my gun was a living object or not, for in the gathering darkness, rocks, reeds, and bushes had assumed the most fantastic shapes. I became confused as to which of them I should direct my aim. At length I resolved to creep from my hiding-place, and for this purpose placed the small leather cushion on which I was seated on my head, and endeavoured to lift the prickly bush above. I was thus engaged when I received a fearful whop upon my head, which knocked me over, bushes and all, while some heavy brute passed over my prostrate form, landing me a prickly cropper upon my own porcupine shield. Off went the gun haphazard, and I scrambled to my feet as best I could.

I was just recovering my senses, when up came the dogs, sniffing and scenting the air. They, however, appeared as bewildered as myself, and at last slunk away between my legs. Napoleon followed, blundering as fast as the darkness would permit him through the deep ravine; and on his inquiry as to what I had fired at, I told him to go to the devil and see! He lit a match and looked into the prickly bush from which I had been so ruthlessly turned out. We found, near the edge of the pool, the deeply-indented footing where some heavy beast had landed on springing from the rocks overhead.

There could be no doubt in our minds that they were made by the leopard I had been waiting for. On Napoleon expressing some doubts as to whether or not the same beast might not be now waiting for us, we left in a most hasty and undignified manner the scene of my late skirmish. The result of my first interview was not of an engaging nature; and I made up my mind that the next time I arranged for a meeting, it should be on terms which, at least, offered more elbow-room.

The great sportsman at the camp was a man called Watson. He had been a keeper in England. He was master of all sorts of dodges for trapping, shooting, and stuffing of game. He had observed, near an abandoned cattle-*kraal* at a neighbouring farm, a large pool of stagnant water, around which he had made out, amid the many marks of wild animals, the spoor of a leopard, which he pretended was the same brute that had given me such a boxing-lesson in the *kloof*. Dix, Watson, and Nap now set to work to sink a hole not far from the pond, around which they placed a circle of bushes. They made, however, such a dense turret, that it was impossible to obtain an entrance into it. I explained to them that the only way for me to gain admittance would be for one of them to be tied with a rope, and then, bodkin-fashion, to be pushed through the prickly bush to make an entrance. This plan, however, did not quite satisfy them.

The only other method of proceeding was to throw their leather jackets on the top of the turret, and to place myself thereon. This pin-cushion was not, however, stout enough, and let the thorns through; so, after several attempts, in which I got severely pricked somewhere for my pains, I gave the setting dodge up. It was finally decided that the turret was to be removed; that we were to station ourselves at various parts of the building, a couple of goats being attached in a prominent place to attract the leopard to the spot, and a volley from us all was to settle the question. In accordance with this suggestion, the next day the goats were brought, and pegged down, as we had previously determined. Dix had also brought some fowls, which he pretended, by their crowing, would greatly enhance the chance of attracting the leopard's attention.

We persisted in this plan for several days, but with so little promise of success, that I thought the odds were more in favour of attracting stray *Kaffirs* towards us, and being made game of ourselves. This not answering my sporting programme, I returned to the original plan of placing myself in the hole, which was sufficiently deep to conceal me; and there, without covering of any sort, to await the advent of any four-footed beast that would kindly come to the rendezvous. On the night of the fourth day of kneeling attention I really saw a leopard slowly approaching the pond. I had an undeniable proof of his nature by the scampering away of several heads of antelope that had been near the pond, and by the loud quacking of a flock of wild-duck then swimming thereon. The brute walked leisurely round the pond until he came to within about twenty yards of the spot where I was lying concealed, when he suddenly disappeared as if by magic.

In vain I strove to discover any signs of his whereabouts. I then partly got out of my hole, and there, kneeling on the edge, I could dimly see his flattened form. Now, what was to be done? He offered no fair mark for my rifle. I was afraid, in that uncertain light, to go nearer him; and he, on his side, decided on not coming nearer me. I passed what seemed to me a very long and *très mauvais quart d'heure* in this anxious state; the night was closing in fast, the moon would not be up until very late, and I really knew not what to do. In this uncertainty I crept backwards limbs is concerned; but their features will not bear the same close inspection. Winsome, coy, and to a certain degree striking when young, they become snappish, coarse, and ungainly as they advance in years.

Noziah, of whom mention has already been made, was far handsomer than the ordinary women of her tribe (Timbuctoo), and betrayed her birth by her stately carriage and the extreme delicacy of her hands and feet. Her mental capacity was equal to that of any untutored woman I ever came in contact with; she understood thoroughly the intricate policy then being carried out at the Cape, the position of the Dutch and English settlers, and the use the *Kaffirs* might make of these two antagonistic interests for their own profit. She also was well aware of the task the missionary was performing, the progress of English civilisation, and the good and evil that it was then bringing into the land. In short, she was a woman capable of undertaking any noble task which Providence in its wisdom might have thought necessary.

General Cathcart now returned from his Basutoland expedition. Macomo and Sandilli had made peace with the British authorities upon terms that neither they nor the colonists could then or afterwards exactly make out. All that seemed perfectly clear was, that when the English Government had made up its mind as to the delimitations of territory, &c., that decision would be duly signified to all interested; and let the terms be as onerous or as arbitrary, as stupid or as wise, as the authorities at home could devise, they had to be accepted.

My corps having no further *raison d'être* was disbanded, and a most flattering general order issued, in which the commander-in-chief stated the following:—

Headquarters, Graham's Town, 22nd March 1853. The Commander-in-chief, in disbanding this corps,— the Waterkloof Rangers,—wishes to convey to its gallant commander, officers, and men, the high estimation in which he holds their services, &c.
(Signed)   A. J. Cloëte,   Quartermaster-General.

On my return towards England I was most kindly greeted at Fort Beaufort with an address, presented to me by the principal inhabitants of the town.

At Graham's Town a similar address was presented to me by Messrs Godlington and Cocks, members of the Legislative Council, and signed by the principal inhabitants of the town and the district around. I afterwards went with these gentlemen to the sea-coast to find out whether or not a safe roadstead for shipping could be established somewhat nearer the town than Port Elizabeth. Being somewhat of a military engineer, this proved an agreeable task; and I was already actively engaged in drawing out plans when the news arrived of the death of a very near relative. This closed all prospect of banquets and receptions, or proposals for new harbours; and I must confess that it was some slight consolation to think that I should not have to present myself at the head of a dinner-table as the honoured guest, to reply to vapid compliments.

At Port Elizabeth another equally gratifying address was presented to me, and what rendered it more pleasing was the fact of its being offered by Mr Deare, Mr Wylde, and other gentlemen, who had so kindly foretold my success as I passed through their town on my way to the front. I stayed a few days at Port Elizabeth, and one morning I walked with some merchants and others on its surf-beaten shore to see how a jetty could be made to facilitate landing (they had heard of my plans concerning another place), for I always had a mania for building that follows like my shadow wherever I go.

I seldom see a spot but I always, in imagination at least, commence building upon it,—not that I care a whit whether it is for myself or another; yet more than one giant is living in *the House that Jack built.*

Wherever I have passed, a road, a bridge, a chapel,—a something, has marked my passage. I once built a jetty in the Bay of Bourgas, betwixt Varna and Constantinople, 147 yards long, 8 yards wide, having 22 feet of water; and on it embarked 45,000 troops, 9400 horses, 140 field-guns, with ample stores, for the

Crimea; and the jetty (which is still standing), and the embarkation above mentioned, all was completed in twelve weeks. It is true I was helped by a British officer. Commodore Eardley Wilmot, of Her Majesty's steamer *Sphinx*, but neither of us got (nor in fact wanted) anything for our pains. The pleasure of the work was sufficient payment. I merely mention these things that the reader may know that I am not a mere amateur soldier, but one who has had a practical knowledge of his work.

As I said above, I was walking on the sea-shore when I was accosted by a good-looking sailor with "Sir, I am a fellow-countryman of yours, and a west-countryman to boot. I should like to shake hands; my name is Sam Rowe, and I hail from Penzance."

I expressed the pleasure, which I really felt, on making his acquaintance. After this he joined us as we proceeded in our examination of the beach. When this was over, while we were returning to the town, Mr Sam Rowe said he wanted a minute's private talk with me. Stepping aside for that purpose, he informed me that he would be happy to take me to Cape Town if I would go in that nice little craft, pointing to a cutter in the bay. He had heard from the town-folks that I was going there, and he thought I should like to sail with him. The vessel was his, and his time too. It was impossible to reply to Mr Rowe's eager offer by refusal, so with a shake of the hand it was arranged there and then.

The conditions were that the vessel was to be mine during the trip; he and his crew, consisting of three men and a boy (his son) were to be at my orders. Of stores there were plenty— fish, poultry, and salted pork, captains' biscuits from Plymouth, bloaters direct from Yarmouth, and real rum from Jamaica. As for the craft herself—named *Mary Jane*, after his little daughter at home—why, nothing afloat, from a St Michael oranger to a fifty-gun frigate, could stand with her in a gale or a breeze. All these things Captain Sam Rowe offered me, and in exchange only required the company of my humble self, and yarns from the seat of war.

it would be strange if it were not; yet in a contrast like the above, it must be confessed that it has, outwardly at least, a rather "Brummagem" look. The Protestantism of Germany, in spite of its dreary aspirations, has a much broader basis. It encourages an untrammelled intercourse between thinkers of all denominations. There is an ebb and flow of ideas going on between it and the older forms of religion in the East which merit the attention of all who follow the outward growth and forms of Christianity.

I have attended a Protestant service in the East where more than half of a large congregation were members of the Greek Church; and of the many members of that community with whom I have come into contact, and with whom I have spoken on the subject of religion, none seemed to dislike, and many seemed to like, the Saxon form of Protestantism as it exists in Transylvania; and I must testify that a better class of men than there produced under this form of religion it would be difficult to find anywhere.

To return from this long digression to my position at Cape Town. My execution of some Hottentot deserters had made me some pious enemies there. Of this I was quite indifferent. The commander-in-chief, who saw one of them strung up to a tree, displayed his approval of the proceeding. I intimated, however, to those who were kindly bestirring themselves to get up an address to me from the inhabitants of Cape Town to leave the matter alone. I had been perfectly satisfied with the recognition of those living near the seat of war, who had had opportunities of seeing the work I had to do, and the way in which I did it.

I now prepared for my return to England. I had several proposals, amongst others, from my friend Captain Sam Rowe, who placed himself and his stout little smack at my disposal. I hardly liked the idea of being cooped up again in so small a space for so long a voyage, al-though I was strongly tempted by the thought of visiting the whole western coast of Africa, as Captain Rowe proposed we should do. I even entertained, for a time, the idea of traversing the whole continent—at all events, of proceeding up the Zambesi, and from thence on to Zanzibar.

But the supposed hostility of the Portuguese authorities to
the last-named trip, which was somewhat confirmed by the
conversations I had with the Portuguese Consul at Cape Town,
prevented me. The trip across the continent was also put off by
the refusal of the Hon. R. C——, who did not wish to go to
such length on a shooting expedition (the only object he had
in view); while I, more ambitiously inclined, had not the means
to make alone so lengthened a journey as a trip across the dark
continent would have been.

After many hesitations, the fortunate arrival of some brother
officers from the seat of war decided the question. We engaged
for ourselves a schooner-yacht called the *Arethusa*, belonging to
a Mr Eade, a London merchant: the only part of the vessel not at
our disposal was the necessary space for a sufficient cargo as ballast. Everything being ready for our departure, we were seated
in the boat that was to convey us to the tight little ship that had
already let go her hold of African ground, and was tacking about
in the bay, bending her white wings to the breeze, seemingly as
eager as ourselves to wend her way to our island-home. There
were many kind *adieus* waved to us from the shore, which the
Arethusa acknowledged by a parting salute from her small mini-
ature guns.

Loud cheers, hurrahs, sham demonstrations—the more boisterous the better, to conceal real parting regret—when, above all
the din, one clear shrill voice pierced my ear as an arrow. "Come
back! come back!" it cried. I looked behind, and there, on the
pier, stood Noziah beckoning me to return to the shore. How
could I? What could I say to her? Never by word or deed had I
wronged her. Often when she looked in a mirror had she told
me that she wished herself dead because her skin was not white
like mine. Her simple faith, however, shamed mine.

When I told her that "*God made us all equal*," her colour ever
rose like a sable shroud between her life and mine. If ever the
dream of making all races one is to be realised, God must do it;
man never can. So the boat went on its way, and I left that dusky

form standing on the narrow pier like a statue of clay.

When the war had come to an end, I had obtained, through the kindness of General Cathcart, an order for a commissariat transport to take Noziah to her brother Sandilli. This conveyance was afterwards sold off and purchased by her. In this she had come to Cape Town.

My agent, Mr H——, upon whom she called the next day as she was leaving the town, wrote and informed me that she had gone back to her home. This was the last I heard of that pure-hearted, innocent African maid.

Once on board I had plenty of interesting matters to think about. I had brought down from the front several wild animals and birds, which I intended for the zoological gardens at home. Amongst others, a springbok, which Mr Mitchell, then director of the gardens in Regent's Park, informed me was the first of that species of antelope that had been seen alive in England.

I also had several birds equally rare, and monkeys, besides sacks of roots, bulbs, and herbs, the spoils of African glades, with which I intended to adorn my own little garden at home.

When all things had been safely stowed away, and night was drawing on, I went to the taffrail, and looking over, thought of the land now sinking in the distance. It is a glorious spot that Cape, which Vasco de Gama called of Good Hope, while he thought of the wonders it contained, as yet unseen by the white man. And so it is still to all those who seek a future for our race: that mighty continent which Grant has lately strode over, and Livingstone claimed for us by there laying down his life. The entire continent must, in my opinion, be yet spread open to us through the Cape of Good Hope.

When I proposed to the Hon. R. C—— the noble task of pioneering the way, I felt that we then stood at the real starting-point. It is useless to seek a passage by wading through the oceans of sandy deserts in effete Northern Africa, when the explorer may recruit his strength, and start almost every day with renewed life, from the fertile unexhausted Cape.

Of settled life there is already a strong and valuable nucleus.

It was only in 1855 that I at last obtained a hearing. Lord Clarendon, to whom I sent a copy of my suggestions as to what England ought to do, wrote me to say that I should no doubt be glad to hear that her Majesty's Government had taken the necessary measures to place the tomb, residence, &c., under the safeguard of the French Government. He did not, however, mention a word of recognition as to its having been done at my suggestion; in fact, on re-reading his letter today, it seems to imply that *he* was the author of the whole affair, and *I* merely a busy-body in the matter.

My correspondence during the conferences held for the signing of the Treaty of Paris will explain many curious, and I may say interesting, details as to this Treaty still undreamt of by the public.

I now turned my attention to the attainment of my long-hoped-for position in the British army; and in this the Duke of Newcastle, then Colonial Minister—who had always taken a warm interest in my welfare, as he did in that of many others—promised to support me to the utmost of his power, in accordance with the deserts of my actual services, and the loud recognition the colonists themselves in their addresses to me had vouchsafed to give. Days and weeks went by without any progress being made in the matter, and I passed my time in travelling between London and Tamworth. Now and then, indeed, I attended a public dinner, at which I made short, confused speeches—for I really never could understand what I had done worth being thanked for; and I only hoped to be enabled, from my past efforts and position acquired, to do something more.

This opportunity, however, the Horse Guards authorities seemed determined not to give me. One day I received a letter from the Colonial Secretary, saying I had better come up to town and place the matter myself before the proper authorities. This was an intense bore to me. If I had rendered any real service it was patent enough to explain itself, but I had an excessive dislike to perform the part of oculist to those who were wilfully blind. However, I submitted so far as to write the usual letter asking for an audience of the Military Secretary. The reply came in due time, and I presented myself at the Horse Guards on the day stated for reception.

My number was twelve; and when it was called out I went to the door leading to the audience-room, and was in the act of entering, when a tall, lanky fellow, coming up quickly from behind, pushed me aside, and thrust himself before me into the room. I was in no good humour at the time, and I have no doubt looked bent on resenting this impertinent act; but before I could reach out my hand to turn this young fellow round and ask for an explanation, Colonel Airey stepped up between us, and said, "Captain Lakeman, let me beg of you to wait for a few minutes outside, for I have some words of importance to communicate to this gentleman."

I felt but little inclined to accede to this wish, and explained that I had as yet no apology for what had taken place. He said he would give me that himself, and again begged me kindly to wait outside.

To this, after some demur, I consented, for I could not readily conceive what prevented the young man in question from giving an excuse for his rudeness, assuming that he had one to offer; so I said, as he was looking from the colonel to me, open-mouthed, without saying a word, "If this gentleman is a foreigner, and cannot speak English, let the matter rest for the moment," and thereupon I left the room. I stayed, kicking my heels for some time outside, strongly tempted to leave, for I felt instinctively nothing good was likely to result from the proposed interview; but I thought of the kind-hearted Duke, and to oblige him I remained. At length my number was called again, and upon entering, the colonel was most off-handed in his communications.

"You see, Captain Lakeman," he said, "the times are looking dark in the East, as you no doubt are aware, and coming events cast their shadows before: much anxiety is felt at the Horse Guards. I have some doubts myself as to whether I shall not throw down the pen and take up the sword. You see blood will tell, and that young gentle-man, who I must say behaved rather abruptly towards you, came also to offer his services at this critical time."

I said, "May I ask you. Colonel, the name of that young man?"

"Oh dear me, yes!" he said; "it was Viscount Forth. You see. Captain Lakeman," he added, "that in times such as these we want the back-bone of the nation, the English aristocracy, to come to the front." (By a curious coincidence this back-bone of the nation did come to the front in the Crimea, in the very first engagement he was in, for he showed it instead of his chest to the Russians as he bolted to Balaklava.) "And I have just presented to him a commission. Now please let me know, Captain Lakeman, what I can do for you."

I was turning over in my mind what answer to give to this polite inquiry, when this usually taciturn military secretary, in seemingly over-flowing spirits, burst out again, with a wave of the hand—

"Oh, it is needless to ask; his Grace has kindly spoken in your behalf, but really I am sorry to say that we have bestowed so many commissions of late, that I think, after all, as you are rich, you had better purchase, and I will do all I can to remove any impediments in the way as to age, &c."

I was then twenty-four. This very kind proposal had such a supremely ridiculous effect on me, that notwithstanding all my efforts to contain myself before so dignified a person as the Military Secretary, I could not help laughing audibly. It did not even occur to me that I ought to make any attempt to conceal my amusement at this ridiculous proposal, so, bowing lowly, I rose and left the room, leaving the somewhat astonished colonel alone in his doubts as to whether, after all, Viscount Forth or myself had the best claims to a commission in Her Majesty's service.

This was the discouraging result of a military education, finished at the best Continental schools, with the further advantage of having accompanied European armies in the field for the sake of instruction; of having placed the modern rifle, at my own expense, in the hands of the British soldier; of showing the use of better accoutrements (my men wore the helmet in 1851); of having been mentioned many times in general orders for gallant conduct in the field, &c., &c. Well, I thought, the sooner this state of affairs is changed the sooner Old England will find better servants.

In this mood I went to report progress in Downing Street. His Grace of Newcastle was kind and considerate as usual, and abused the Horse Guards as heartily as the British radical, and finally left me to consult with Mr E———, his private secretary, as to what now remained to be done to meet the views of the colonists concerning a recognition of my services to them.

In the present state of affairs nothing suitable seemed to present itself; a civil employment abroad—the only gift at the disposal of the Colonial Office—did not meet my views; so, after a lengthened confab, I returned to my *lares* and *penates*, and awaited events.

CHAPTER 15

Conclusion

Events came rapidly enough. Those shadows in the East at which Colonel Airey had been throwing his pen, and was now preparing his sword to demolish, were thickening fast. A mission was offered to me to go to Constantinople, which I eagerly accepted, and in September 1853 I left England for the East. On my arrival there I was sent by Lord Stratford de Redcliffe to Gallipoli. I made a lengthy report to show the uselessness of that spit of land as a place of rendezvous for the English and French to fight the Russians, then hundreds of miles away across the Balkans and the Danube.

Gallipoli is a point that may be used to threaten Asia, but not Europe. As such it was used by the Galli or Gauls—hence its name. I exposed the fact that an army disembarking for the purpose of repelling an invader, which the Russian army was, lost all the prestige of success by preparing defences in case of retreat, and the fortifying of Gallipoli meant nothing else. It seemed almost cowardly thus to begin when the Turks alone were meeting the Russians in the open field. After Lord Stratford had received this report, he sent me further directions to visit the whole length of the Dardanelles and investigate the military and political influence they would possess in the East, supposing a war took place between England and Russia.

These instructions I followed out, and afterwards returned to Constantinople along the shores of the Sea of Marmora, giving further details concerning the entire coast. His lordship was so satisfied with the manner in which I had performed my task that he gave me immediately another to perform. I was sent on board H.M.S. the *Valorous*, Captain Loring, with a dragoman of the Embassy (Mr Sarel), to Varna, from whence I was to visit all the fortresses on the Danube, to report on their actual state and future importance, and to furnish a description of the Turkish army then in Bulgaria.

On landing at Varna, I found that a report on that place would be useless, as Colonel Neale, then Her Majesty's Consul there, was putting the last touch to a most able account of its importance and real value. The Colonel had seen fighting whilst employed in the Spanish Legion under brave General Evans, and was as competent in wielding the pen as the sword.

From Varna we proceeded to Schumla, and a bitterly cold trip it was. I must here explain that I had left Constantinople in an evening costume in the following manner: At a *soiree* held at the Embassy at which I had the honour to assist. Lord Stratford, to whom that same day I had given in my report concerning the Dardanelles, came from his study into the room and said he wanted me to make a similar report on the Danube, and that I must start directly. He had just spoken to Captain Loring of the *Valorous* on the subject, who had already left the Embassy for his vessel. Steam was already up, and the sooner I left the better.

As for clothes, I might have anything in his own wardrobe. Without more ado I took a greatcoat belonging to his lordship, which I still possess as a reminiscence of one of the greatest men England ever sent to represent her.

Thus accoutred I went on board, Mr Sarel following much in the same style of attire. When on board. Captain Loring kindly offered any part of his outfit for my use, but no number of reefs would bring them to a suitable shape on my then slender form; and Colonel Neale's short hose were so stumpy and baggy as to make me look like a Blue-coat boy under the trailing garment of Lord Stratford: so I declined all these proffered masqueradings, and got on my Tartar post-boy charger on my way to Schumla, bundled up in such rolls of hay round my legs and arms as to make my little nag more inclined to eat than to carry me.

Poor Sarel was in a still worse plight than myself. I at all events had been well hardened in the saddle, while he had only been accustomed to the soft chairs at the Embassy, and soon sat on the leather of his seat as though it had been the pigskin of the tenderest sucking-pig in Bulgaria.

Thus we proceeded in a rather undignified fashion up the Deona Valley, through Peveda and Batschesci to Schumla. There I saw Omar Pasha, and after two or three interviews, cemented an intimacy with him that the efforts of none could afterwards break until he left this world.

Omar had all the talents in him of which great men are made, but he had also the dominant failing of the weakest—namely, that of an unbeliever. It was at Schumla that I had the first opportunity of seeing the sterling worth and the vices of the Turkish army, of which Omar was so fitting a commander and representative chief. Here I saw men who lately, panic-stricken, had run away from a few harmless Russian scouts *on the other side of the Danube*, now patiently dragging, with frost-bitten feet and hands, big siege-guns on sledges through snow as a mere matter of ordinary duty. Tall, sturdy, smiling countenances, with death's cold hand already upon them. But I shall not enlarge on these scenes for the present.

I visited Schumla in question, and returned in the good ship *Valorous* to Constantinople. This city, which an Englishman gave his name to (for Constantine the Great was not only British-born, but his mother, the great St Helena, was the daughter of a remarkable king of Essex), was to me a place of wonder: my eyes were more occupied in feasting on its marvels, than my thoughts in working out its future.

The men of the Embassy were as remarkable as their chief—the Smythes, the Allisons, the Brodies, and the Pisanis, were a bright nucleus of men any nation might be proud of. Neither were the representatives of the real antagonists, Russia and France, much below them—the Aussicks, the Menschikoffs, were no ordinary men.

117

My mission being ended I returned to England, and on arrival found that my report had created more anxiety than satisfaction.

Whatever the world may say or think about those then actually in power, I found them to be possessed of only erroneous preconceptions and to be influenced by indecision. As I unfolded to Lord Raglan the real state of affairs, he kept nervously twitching the stump of his arm, and looked more like a victim going to be sacrificed on the altar of duty, than a general prepared to take the command of an army.

I was thanked for what I had done, but that was all I got for my pains. True, Colonel Airey called me always Captain; but as this was a mere act of courtesy, just as two years afterwards he called me General when in the Crimea, I naturally placed no more value on it than it deserved. I hope, however, that he will read my future description of that campaign, and explain by what misconception he needlessly caused so many thousands of British soldiers to go through such an amount of bitter suffering.

At this time I was offered a knighthood, but refused it as being of no military value to me. Another mission was then proposed, which I accepted. Russia and France seemed determined to seize each other by the throat, in their dispute as to which of them had the right to paint the Holy Sepulchre, and to hold the keys of that tomb which the apostles found empty.

Lord Stratford was looking on as arbitrator. His better judgement was with Russia, but his bias against her; his grand intellect swayed to and fro in his efforts to reconcile both. Some of his despatches at this momentous time are the grandest specimens of diplomatic correspondence to be found in the English language. To those who were cognisant of the tortuous intricacies of the Eastern question, the truth, the energy, the flashes of genius amidst obscure renderings that are therein found, are something truly wonderful.

Had he willed it, at this time, the war would not have taken place; but his great mind at last wearied, and reeled under the burden of holding the balance aloof in such weighty matters; and from being judge he became advocate, thinking, perhaps, that the shells might remain to Russia and France, whilst England should have the oyster. This could not be right, for the British Government had no perception of the duty that was incumbent on possession. Its actions reminded me of what I had then recently witnessed in the Turkish provinces. There *beys* or governors were good enough in themselves, and to those of the same creed, but they lived and haughtily prospered on the vices and failings of those whom they governed.

Parents often kept their children, or children their parents, in prison, to satisfy any pique of the moment, or persistent desire to wrong one another. At Silivri, ancient Silymbria, a town of Roumelia, on the Sea of Marmora, containing about 8000 inhabitants, I turned out of prison upwards of sixty persons, who had been kept in durance vile by the governor on the daily payment of so much per head, according to the rank of the incarcerated, for no crime whatever, but simply to satisfy the grudge of persons with whom they were at enmity.

A Nicolai Bogdan, a wealthy tradesman of the town, had imprisoned his own mother to gratify the spite of his wife for some supposed family wrongs; and as the poor old woman left the prison, where she had been confined for the last four years, squalid in her filth and rags, Ahmed Bey, the governor, asked me if such a dog of a Christian, as Bogdan was, deserved the attention of Lord Stratford. In this observation lay the gist of all the evil of the time.

The Whig Government, more or less subservient to the Manchester school of politics, wanted, like the governor of Silivri, to prosper in a worldly point of view, but did not wish to assume any moral obligation. So long as goods were sold they did not care anything about the buyer personally, or as to where his money came from, provided he did not become bankrupt. They were equally indifferent as to whom fell the task of paying twelve *per cent* interest on the loans they so freely offered to the Turk, forcing him to greater and more relentless exactions on the poor Christian taxpayer for the repayment.

Such policy is as selfish as that of a French Communard, whose motto is, "*After us the Deluge;*" and the deluge *did* come, sweeping away the prosperity and comfort of thousands and thousands of English families who had trusted to the positive indebtedness of the British Government to supervise and direct those to whom they otherwise would not have trusted their hard-earned savings.

It is useless to speak of *hatti-humayoums, irades*, or any other devices of ambassadors, signed by a time-serving *Sultan* for the regeneration of his subjects. Local laws such as these, if applied to the people themselves, may fulfil all their requirements; but foreign suggestions and foreign pressure require foreign subjects, which native subjects who are worthy the name will never become. Neither can you regenerate a nation by the mere force of will, nor by force of arms. The people must have an innate feeling of willing participation to render reforms desirable.

I have had, whilst governor of the district of Bourgas, a sack brought to me by a Bulgarian peasant, which contained the head of his own child, murdered by brigands before his eyes; yet that peasant, who was mayor of his own village, and had ample means of at least making an effort to save it, had never lifted a finger in its behalf, but now came to me for assistance towards payment of the ransom he had promised to save another child he had at home. I ask, what laws could regenerate the conduct of that man? Parental love could not even arouse him to his duty towards his own flesh and blood! What chance would foreign devices have to move him?

I do not cite this as a solitary case, but as one of many similar examples of degradation which weigh upon a large portion of the population in Turkey. I have more than once seen a Turk maltreating a Christian. I have had the instrument taken out of the hand of the offender and placed in the hands of the stricken, then, standing over both, have insisted upon retaliation. But this was too abstruse a method for the perception of a Bulgarian. If, thought he, no doubt, I could really help him, why not let him *murder* the Turk? As for beating, that would still leave his foe alive, and after my departure the Turk would thrash him worse than ever. What the Bulgarian told me in 1854 is applicable now—

Leave the Christian alone in the hands of the Turk, and he will be more despised and ill-governed than ever.

The clergy in the East, as might be readily supposed, offer no fixed standard of morality to guide the masses, as the following, among many other cases brought to my knowledge, will readily prove. When the Emperor Nicholas of Russia died, I was then in command of Western Roumelia; and the clergy of the district, headed by the Metropolitan of Adrianople, came officially to ask of me, as a Christian *Pasha*, to be allowed to celebrate a Mass for the repose of the Emperor's soul. The ostensible reason given for this act of public gratitude was the many acts of solicitude the dead Emperor had shown for their church: scarcely an ornament on their altars, even to the very canonical costumes which they then had on their backs, but they were indebted to him for.

This outward demonstration imposed so much upon me that I told the Metropolitan, and the other bishops with him, that if they were so much indebted, why did they not, by some overt act beyond spiritual regard, show their acknowledgments? The successor of him whom they so deeply deplored had ascended the throne. France, England, and Turkey were in the field against him, and he had not a friend in the world—not even Austria, who owed her very existence to his father—that would say a word or lift a finger in his behalf. Now, at this solemn moment for the orthodox church, a universal display in favour of Alexander might so impress the Allies as to eventually bring about a close of the war without too much sorrow and suffering on the part of Russia.

The Metropolitan replied, "We have nothing to offer Russia alive; when she is dead, all we can do is to offer up prayers for her."

So much for Christian gratitude in the East—and be it re-marked that these Vladicas and Popas were not all Greeks, but many of them Bulgarians.

I was now on the point of leaving England once more without the slightest notice having been taken of the recommendations of General Sir Harry Smith, General Cathcart, or of the colonists regarding my services, when it was suggested by Lord Clarendon, whom I was going specially to serve, that some sort of handle to my name would increase the chances of my being useful to him. The letter of the noble statesman on this subject, which is still in my possession, would merit a place, and that not a low one, amidst a collection of jokes of the period. Its only fault is that it makes one laugh on the wrong side of the face. This parental solicitude of the Foreign Office towards one of its adopted little children aroused me to the necessity of belonging to some established English institution.

The Horse Guards, where I begged my new guardian still to leave me, had refused to receive me without payment. As a *pis aller*, it was decided that I should be sent to Windsor Castle; and I must say that, after all my late tossings about, I had reason to be gratified at last, for I breathed much more freely there than in Downing Street—and I was, b-sides, much more kindly treated.

The journey to Windsor Castle was a pleasant one. I was seated between Lord Palmerston and Lord Aberdeen; and although the Duke of Newcastle had assured me that Lord Palmerston was always so much behind time as never to see fish on his own table, yet he managed to come in very strong with the *roast* for Lord Aberdeen before we got to Windsor. The quiet old Scotch-man seemed more than once on the point of "spitting" out a not over-polite expletive in reply, but, on reflection, he always managed to bolt it. The two presented such a contrast, that it appeared to me, a youngster, incredible that they could occupy the same political level. The former amused himself by pumping me out; the latter required almost a force-pump to get anything into him.

The result might be the same, but the operation was quite different. I took, however, special pains during the journey to instil into the mind of this kilted-petticoat authority that, although I looked so young, I was really no novice in the art of war. He was to be my respondent, or warrantor, for my qualifications as a knight-bachelor, whatever that may mean.

At length we arrived at the castle. The ministers went to attend a Cabinet Council. It looked more as if they had been engaged on some parish business than on the affairs of the world. I was left alone to promenade up and down a long corridor, lined with my predecessors in glory—knights-dummies in armour. I was getting tired of my monologues with these iron-jawed gentry, and beginning to feel some uncomfortable twinges from an inward monitor not always easily appeased after a country ride, when the young Duke of Brabant, the present king of the Belgians, came up to me and asked if I was Captain Lakeman from the Cape. He said that the Duke of Newcastle had told him of my presence; and he added, I would no doubt easily excuse his anxiety to know all about the Dutch colonists, in whom his father also took the warmest interest.

I was relating to him, in as few words as possible, all I knew about the sturdy Dutchmen, with whom I also claimed a common descent, when a most solemn-looking personage came up and told me to follow him. After a warm shake-hands, which the young duke honoured me with, I followed the gentleman in black as gravely as though this had been my last farewell on earth. He led the way to a small side door, and opening it as a church-beadle opens a pew, beckoned me to enter. I bowed, and walked in. It was a small, oak-panelled room, in the middle of which stood a lady surrounded by sedate-looking men. I felt as if a mistake had been made,—that I had got into the manorial enclosure instead of the strangers' pew,—and was on the point of bowing myself out again, in the humblest way possible, as a proof of my unintentional intrusion, when the lady mentioned smiled so kindly that I left off bowing and walked further on.

There was no necessity to tell me now that I was in the presence of the Queen. *I felt that I was.* Whatever may be often thought nowadays of "such divinity as doth hedge mon-

123

archs," I for my part was ready at once to acknowledge that fealty to England's ruler which, hitherto, I had only offered to the dear country itself. After a few words had passed, a cushion was brought and laid before me, and then another, on which there was a heavy-looking sword.

Someone behind me whispered that I was to kneel—an operation by no means agreeable to a man before company. This I somewhat awkwardly did, and so remained, with my face bent towards Her Majesty's feet, expecting every moment to feel the weight of the sword on my shoulder to indicate that the ceremony had begun, but nothing came. There was a dead silence. So I looked up and saw the Queen holding up the sword and directing an inquiring glance towards some one behind my back. Whoever that person was, he seemed to be a long time in answering. It was the Earl of Aberdeen. It was evident to me that Her Majesty could not hold the sword over my head much longer. I asked what was wanted.

"Your Christian name," Her Majesty said.

"Stephen," I replied; and down came the sword, missing the shoulder and striking the cushion. The ceremony, however, was complete without that, for Her Majesty immediately said, "Arise, Sir Stephen," and held out her hand to kiss. I did kiss it, and felt in doing so that she had not many in her wide realm who would serve her more devotedly than I if necessity required it.

The cushions were removed; the Queen graciously smiled to all around and left the room, and we retired together through the long corridor before mentioned. I was standing near the entrance to the castle door whilst the Earl of Clarendon was lighting a cigar, when the Duke of Newcastle rejoined us, and said, "Allow me to congratulate you as Sir Stephen Lakeman, and as to having your head still on. I thought at one time Her Majesty was going to cut it off."

"Ah," said Lord Clarendon, puffing away at his cigarette, which I thought extremely unbecoming in the castle, "if the Queen had given it a whack it would have done it good."

"Just as it might do your lordship to whack out your cigarette," I replied. I had, within the last few days, taken a sudden dislike to his lordship, which, however unaccountable at the time, was a true presentiment of our future relations. His Grace of Newcastle took me by the arm and led me away. He at the same time informed me that I was to remain at the castle: a certain person, whom he pointed out, would attend to my wants, and I might freely answer any questions that would be put to me during the afternoon.

When I returned to town that night, I was grateful for the honours that had been bestowed upon me at the request of the Cape colonists.

www.ingramcontent.com/pod-product-compliance
Lightning Source LLC
Chambersburg PA
CBHW031858090426
42741CB00005B/552